Reply

TO:

THE ADVISORY OPINION OF 9 JULY 2004
—— IN THE MATTER OF THE ——

LEGAL CONSEQUENCES OF THE CONSTRUCTION OF A WALL IN THE OCCUPIED PALESTINIAN TERRITORY

—— AS SUBMITTED BY THE ——
INTERNATIONAL COURT OF JUSTICE

Eli E. Hertz

Myths and Facts, Inc.
New York

To my wife Marilyn and my children Etie, Mala and Danny,
thank you for your love and support

Published by:
Myths and Facts, Inc.
PO Box 941, Forest Hills, NY 11375

Myths and Facts, Inc. is a tax-exempt organization under section 501(c)(3) of the Internal Revenue Code ("IRC") and all contributions to it are deductible as charitable contributions.

www.MythsandFacts.org
eMail Address: contact@MythsandFacts.org

Library of Congress Catalog Number: 2005921657

ISBN: 0-9741804-0-8

Printed in the United States of America

Eli E. Hertz, Editor-in-Chief, Writer and Publisher
Daniella Ashkenazy, Chief Researcher and Writer

Cover design by Nick Moscovitz

Table of Contents

Introduction

"After a sharp rise in Palestinian *terror attacks* in the spring of 2002" the Government of Israel called for the construction of a Barrier in parts of the West Bank. (UN GA, Resolution ES-10/248.)

On 21 October 2003, the UN General Assembly adopted resolution ES-10/13, that among others: "*Demands* that Israel stop and reverse the construction of the wall in the Occupied Palestinian territory, including in and around East Jerusalem."

On 24 November 2003, the UN General Assembly adopted Resolution ES-10/248, concluding that "Israel is not in compliance with the Assembly's demand that it 'stop and reverse the construction of the wall in the Occupied Palestinian Territory.'"

On 3 December 2003, the UN General Assembly adopted Resolution ES-10L.16, to [among others] "request the International Court of Justice ... to urgently render an advisory opinion" on the legal consequences arising from he construction of the wall being built by Israel.

On 9 July 2004, the International Court of Justice delivered its Advisory Opinion on the "LEGAL CONSEQUENCES OF THE CONSTRUCTION OF A WALL IN THE OCCUPIED PALESTINIAN TERRITORY."

For the sake of safeguarding history and in honour of justice – I **Reply.**

"A recommendation's significance will not least depend on the moral authority of the adopting organ. Only the maintenance of high and impartial standards of decision-making in the international organ will endow its recommendations with persuasive force for all sectors of the international community. The application of politically motivated double standards or the use of general resolutions to champion positions in political quarrels are liable to undermine the credibility of the international organ even in areas of relative agreement."[1]

---

[1] More than two decades ago, in his volume "Israel and Palestine: Assault on the Law of Nations," jurist Professor Julius Stone quoted a warning issued by Professor Schreuer in 1977 regarding the state of international law, written against the backdrop of a growing tendency within the General Assembly to adopt double standards and the waning credibility of the General Assembly's resolutions as a result. Schreuer's words are particularly relevant today vis-à-vis the International Court of Justice. More about Professor Christoph H. Schreuer see:

http://www.austria.org/oldsite/oct95/quit.htm. (11028)

This document uses extensive links via the Internet. If you experience a broken link, please note the 5 digit number (xxxxx) at the end of the URL and use it as a Keyword in the Search Box at www.MEfacts.com.

1 Testimony Testifying Against Israel

The ICJ invites a series of anti-Israeli terrorist organizations that openly champion and justifies use of force and terrorism as a means of achieving their objectives as "likely to be able to furnish information on the question submitted to the Court"[2]

It is revealing just whom the ICJ believed could *contribute* information under its limited, fact-finding apparatus of written affidavits and oral presentations.

The ICJ heard testimony from the PLO, the Organization of Islamic Conference (OIC), and the Arab League, while refusing to hear any input from the Israeli victims of terrorism.

The ICJ approved requests from the League of Arab States (which is officially in a state of war with Israel), and the Organization of the

---

[2] "Legal consequences of the construction of a wall in the Occupied Palestinian Territory", 9 July 2004, paragraph 6. [10908]

Islamic Conference (OIC) to participate.[3] The ICJ's decision to honor the requests of these two Arab 'international bodies' (i.e. accepting that they have something to contribute to the question at hand) is allowed under Article 66, Clause 3 of the ICJ's Charter. Yet the decision to invite them is in stark contrast with the fact that the ICJ did not consider it fitting and proper to invite the Organization of Casualties of Terror Acts in Israel (Almagor) to present evidence – a step offered under Article 66, Clause 2 of its own Charter, which makes provisions for its own judicial procedures:

> "To … notify any state entitled to appear before the Court or international organization considered by the Court … as likely to be able to furnish information on the question."

A request on the part of Israeli terror victims' families to participate in oral hearings was rejected by the ICJ on the eve of oral hearings on the grounds that the families do not represent a country and therefore should not take part in the hearings.[4]

This was doubly ironic, for prior to this the ICJ decided in the Order of its docket, Resolution 2 (December 19, 2003) that it is fitting and proper for the ICJ to permit 'Palestine' – which does not represent a country – to "submit to the Court a written statement on the question … taking into account the fact that the General Assembly has granted Palestine a special status of observer and that the latter is co-sponsor of the draft resolution requesting the advisory opinion."[5]

Dr. Pieter H. F. Bekker, a member of the American Society of International Law and former staff lawyer at the ICJ, dryly described the

---

[3] "OIC at Hague: Link between suicide attacks, Israeli 'terror'" at: http://www.jafi.org.il/education/actual/conflict/fence/6.html. (11352)

[4] "ICJ rejects terror victim's families participation," *Jerusalem Post*, February 21, 2004 at: http://www.jpost.com/servlet/Satellite?pagename=JPost/JPArticle/Printer&cid=1077351468319. (11353)

[5] Order 19 December, 2003, at: http://www.mefacts.com/cache/pdf/wallruling_/11354.pdf. (11354)

This document uses extensive links via the Internet. If you experience a broken link, please note the 5 digit number (xxxxx) at the end of the URL and use it as a Keyword in the Search Box at www.MEfacts.com.

ICJ's decision to invite a non-state - "a novelty."[6] In fact, it is not only unprecedented; it is also a travesty of justice. The ICJ 'hid' behind a decision taken by a patently anti-Israel body that in 1974 endowed the PLO with unprecedented 'observer status' – a terrorist conglomerate that only two years earlier had murdered 11 Israelis at the Munich Olympics[7] and whose UN-sponsored website to this very day features the "Palestinian Charter" calling for the destruction of Israel by armed struggle.[8]

Taking the 'fence issue' to the International Court of Justice was a controversial step from the start. The voting pattern in the General Assembly on the resolution to request an advisory opinion clearly reflects this. The resolution passed the General Assembly, but not with the typical near-unanimous anti-Israel vote: it even failed to receive an absolute majority among 191 member states. There were 90 in favor, 8 against and 74 (!) abstentions, including most of Europe.[9] 19 delegations didn't even show up to vote.[10]

According to Article 66 of the "International Court of Justice's Charter," "… any state[s] [are] entitled to appear before the Court." Nevertheless, one is struck by the fact that 23 out of the 26 states who chose to present affidavits are categorized as "Not Free" by the human rights monitoring

---

[6]   Pieter H. F. Bekker, "the UN General Assembly Requests a World Court Advisory Opinion on Israel's Separation Barrier," American Society of International Law, December 2003, at: http://www.asil.org/insights/insigh121.htm. (11355)

[7]   This and a host of other atrocities, including a 1970 attack on an Israeli elementary school bus that killed 12 children and adults. For details of the Munich massacre, see: http://www.palestinefacts.org/pf_1967to1991_munich.php. (11356)

[8]   See "Palestine National Charter 1968," at: http://www.pna.gov.ps/Government/gov/plo_Charter.asp. (10366) There is no 'revised text' of the Charter, as promised in 1993 – not on this website or anywhere else.

[9]   Saul Singer, "Delegitimizing Israel," *National Review* at: http://nationalreview.com/script/printpage.asp?ref=/comment/singer200401230908.asp. (11357)

[10]   Pieter H. F. Bekker, "the UN General Assembly Requests a World Court Advisory Opinion on Israel's Separation Barrier," American Society of International Law, December 2003, at: http://www.asil.org/insights/insigh121.htm. (11355)

This document uses extensive links via the Internet. If you experience a broken link, please note the 5 digit number (xxxxx) at the end of the URL and use it as a Keyword in the Search Box at www.MEfacts.com.

organization, Freedom House. Some states are rated as the worse offenders of human rights for which:

> "Political rights are absent or virtually nonexistent as a result of the extremely oppressive nature of the regime or severe oppression in combination with civil war. States and territories in this group may also be marked by extreme violence or warlord rule that dominates political power in the absence of an authoritative, functioning central government."[11]

The 26 states include: Algeria, Bahrain, Bangladesh, Brunei Darussalam, Comoros, Cuba, Djibouti, Egypt, Indonesia, Jordan, Kuwait, Lebanon, Malaysia, Mauritania, Morocco, Namibia, Oman, Qatar, Saudi Arabia, Senegal, Somalia, South Africa, Sudan, Tunisia, United Arab Emirates, Yemen and 'Palestine' – all of whom submitted scathing 'finger pointing' affidavits regarding Israel's conduct. A full quarter of the briefs were from entities that do not even recognize Israel's right to exist or have diplomatic relations with Israel.[12]

What other entities were allowed to present affidavits? Clause 2 of Article 66 of the ICJ's Charter cites that:

> "The Registrar shall also, by means of a special and direct communication, notify any state entitled to appear before the Court or international organization considered by the Court … as likely to be able to furnish information on the question."

It is most incongruous that the ICJ, 'sticking strictly to its mandate' repeats time and again the "inadmissibility of the acquisition of territory by war" (out of context) but sees nothing wrong with accepting testimony from entities that refuse to recognize Israel, oppose compromise, and justify support for or employ terrorism: the PLO, Fatah, the Arab League and the Organization of Islamic States.

---

[11] Freedom House, an NGO founded nearly sixty years ago by Eleanor Roosevelt, monitors the degree of freedom accorded citizens of various countries according to various parameters, and classifies countries accordingly. For the full report see: http://www.freedomhouse.org/research/survey2004.htm. (10783)

[12] Cuba, Indonesia, Kuwait, Lebanon, Republic of Korea. Malaysia, Pakistan, Saudi Arabia, Sudan, Syria and Yemen submitted briefs, but have refused to recognize Israel.

This document uses extensive links via the Internet. If you experience a broken link, please note the 5 digit number (xxxxx) at the end of the URL and use it as a Keyword in the Search Box at www.MEfacts.com.

Fatah - the main faction of the PLO to which Arafat belonged and was its founding member - displays its constitution, a publicly accessible document, on its website.[13] It calls under Article 12 for the

> "Complete liberation of Palestine, and eradication of Zionist economic, political, military and cultural existence."

The next Fatah Constitutional Article calls for:

> "Establishing an independent democratic state with complete sovereignty on all Palestinian lands, and Jerusalem as its capital city, and protecting the citizens' legal and equal rights without any racial or religious discrimination."

As for how it will achieve its goals, Fatah's constitution minces no words:

> "Armed struggle is a strategy and not a tactic, and the Palestinian Arab People's armed revolution is a decisive factor in the liberation fight and in uprooting the Zionist existence, and this struggle will not cease unless the Zionist state is demolished and Palestine is completely liberated."

In the PLO's testimony to the ICJ, which appears in paragraph 115 of the opinion, the organization claims that the Barrier

> "… severs the territorial sphere over which the Palestinian people are entitled to exercise their right of self-determination and constitutes a violation of the legal principle prohibiting the acquisition of territory by the use of force."

The ICJ addresses this charge with all seriousness.

The ICJ decided, in accordance with Article 66 of its Statute, that those two 'international organizations' were likely to be able to *furnish information* on the question submitted to the ICJ. The Court simply warps the intent of the ICJ's mandate which allows international organizations to testify by allowing the League of Arab States and the Organization of the Islamic Conference to present affidavits, ignoring that these two organizations champion the use of violence and defy in word and deed, 'the inadmissibility of use of violence.'

---

[13] Fateh Online, at: http://www.fateh.net/e_public/constitution.htm#Goals. (10910)

This document uses extensive links via the Internet. If you experience a broken link, please note the 5 digit number (xxxxx) at the end of the URL and use it as a Keyword in the Search Box at www.MEfacts.com.

It is illuminating to examine a sample of their records of conduct and public policy statements.

The record of the League of Arab States' resolutions since the founding of the Arab League in 1945 is hardly a model for peaceful settlement of disputes in the spirit of the United Nations. For instance, prior to and following the establishment of the Jewish state, it took the following steps, a partial list of those which are publicly archived:[14]

- In December 1945 the Arab League launched a boycott of 'Zionist goods' that continues to this day.[15]

- In June 1946 it established the Higher Arab Committee to "coordinate efforts with regard to Palestine," a radical body that led and coordinated attempts to wipe Israel off the map.[16]

- In December 1946, it rejected the first Palestine partition plans, reaffirming "that Palestine is a part of the Arab motherland."[17]

- In October 1947 (prior to the vote on Resolution 181) it reasserted the necessity for military preparations along Arab borders to "defending Palestine."[18]

---

[14] Listing of the Arab League sessions covering the League sessions between 4 June 1945 to 17 November 1957 can be found at: http://faculty.winthrop.edu/haynese/mlas/ALSessions.html. (11358)

[15] Session: 2, Cairo, Egypt. Resolution 16 (2 December 1945), "The Boycott of Zionist Goods and Products" (Khalil, 2:161) - plans made to establish a committee to enforce the boycott." (11358)

[16] Session 4, Bludan, Syria, Resolution 82 (12 June 1946), "The Higher Arab Executive Committee" (Khalil, 2:162) - Establish the body to coordinate efforts with regard to Palestine. (11358)

[17] Ibid.

[18] Session: 7, Cairo, Egypt, Resolution 181 (9 October 1947), "Defending Palestine" (Khalil, 2:164-65) - Reassertion of the necessity for military preparations along Arab borders. (11358)

This document uses extensive links via the Internet. If you experience a broken link, please note the 5 digit number (xxxxx) at the end of the URL and use it as a Keyword in the Search Box at www.MEfacts.com.

- In February 1948 it approved "a plan for political, military, and economic measures to be taken in response to the Palestine crisis."[19]

- In October 1948 it rejected the UN partition plan for Palestine adopted by the General Assembly in Resolution 181.[20]

On May 15, 1948 – as the regular forces of Jordan, Egypt, Syria and Lebanon invaded Israel to 'restore law and order,' the Arab League issued a lengthy document entitled "Declaration on the Invasion of Palestine." In it, the Arab States drew attention to:

> "… the injustice implied in this solution [affecting] the right of the people of Palestine to immediate independence … declared the Arabs' rejection of [Resolution 181]" which the League said "would not be possible to carry it out by peaceful means, and that its forcible imposition would constitute a threat to peace and security in this area" and claimed that the "security and order in Palestine have become disrupted" due to the "aggressive intentions and the imperialistic designs of the Zionists" and "the Governments of the Arab States, as members of the Arab League, a regional organization … view the events taking place in Palestine as a threat to peace and security in the area as a whole. … Therefore, as security in Palestine is a sacred trust in the hands of the Arab States, and in order to put an end to this state of affairs … the Governments of the Arab States have found themselves compelled to intervene in Palestine."[21]

The Secretary General of the Arab League, Azzam Pasha, was less diplomatic and far more candid. With no patience for polite or veiled language, on the same day Israel declared its independence on May 14th, 1948, at a Cairo press conference reported the next day in the *New York Times,* Pasha repeated the Arabs' "intervention to restore law and order" revealing:

---

[19] Session: 8, Cairo, Egypt, February 1948, Council approved plan for political, military, and economic measures to be taken in response to the Palestine crisis, including withholding petroleum concessions and other possible sanctions against countries aiding the Zionists. (11358)

[20] Session: 9, Cairo, Egypt, October 1948, rejection of partition plan for Palestine. (11358)

[21] For the full text of the Arab League declaration on the invasion of Palestine - 15 May 1948 see Israel Ministry of Foreign Affairs at: http://www.mefacts.com/cache/html/wall-ruling_/11359.htm. (11359)

"This will be a war of extermination and a momentous massacre which will be spoken of like the Mongolian massacres and the Crusades."

The League of Arab States continued to oppose peace after the war:

- In 15 July 1948 UN Security Council adopted Resolution 54 calling on Arab aggression to stop: "Taking into consideration that the Provisional Government of Israel has indicated its acceptance in principle of a prolongation of the truce in Palestine; that the States members of the Arab League have rejected successive appeals of the United Nations Mediator, and of the Security Council in its resolution 53 (1948) of 7 July 1948, for the prolongation of the truce in Palestine; and that there has consequently developed a renewal of hostilities in Palestine, ..."[22]

- In October 1949 the Arab League declared that negotiation with Israel by any Arab state would be in violation of Article 18 of the Arab League.[23]

- In April 1950 it called for severance of relations with any Arab State which engaged in relations or contacts with Israel and prohibited Member states from negotiating unilateral peace with Israel.[24]

- In March 1979 it suspended Egypt's membership in the League (retroactively) from the date of its signing a peace treaty with Israel.[25]

---

[22] UN Security Council S/RES/54 (1948), 15 July 1948, at: http://domino.un.org/UNISPAL.NSF/0/2e2bcb7cbafd9b70852560c2005b5eec?OpenDocument. (10894)

[23] Session: 11, Resolution 250, October 1949, Cairo, Egypt, Declared that any member State negotiating with Israel would be in violation of Article 18 of the Arab League Pact. (11358)

[24] Session: 12, Resolution 312 (13 April 1950) Called for severance of relations with any Arab State, which engaged in relations or contacts with Israel. (11358)

[25] Session: 70, March 1979, Bagdad, Iraq, Resolution to recommend severance of political and diplomatic relations with Egypt. (11358)

This document uses extensive links via the Internet. If you experience a broken link, please note the 5 digit number (xxxxx) at the end of the URL and use it as a Keyword in the Search Box at www.MEfacts.com.

More recently, in the Beirut Declaration of March 27-28, 2002, adopted at the height of Palestinian suicide attacks, the Arab League declared:

> "We, the kings, presidents, and emirs of the Arab states meeting in the Council of the Arab League Summit in Beirut, capital of Lebanon ... have conducted a thorough assessment of the developments and challenges ... relating to the Arab region and, more specifically, to the occupied Palestinian territory. With great pride, we followed the Palestinian people's intifada and valiant resistance. ... We address a greeting of pride and honour to the Palestinian people's steadfastness and valiant intifada against the Israeli occupation and its destructive war machine. We greet with honour and pride the valiant martyrs of the intifada ..."[26]

This organization, which has systematically opposed and blocked peace efforts for 60 years, and is in a declared state-of-war with Israel, and more recently, proudly and publicly supports the deeds of suicide bombers (*shahids*, or 'martyrs' in Arabic), is now deemed by the International Court of Justice to have something significant to contribute regarding the propriety of Israel's security barrier.

Another 'welcome participant' in the ICJ's proceedings was the Organization of the Islamic Conference. The OIC recently held a conference in Malaysia prior to the issuance of the ICJ opinion, dedicated to refuting the connection between the Muslim world and terrorism. In an editorial in the *Washington Post* ("Death Wish," April 4, 2002)[27] the stunned editors of the paper noted the nature of this organization and its agenda:

> "57 assembled states adopted a resolution that specifically rejected the idea that Palestinian 'resistance' to Israel has anything to do with terrorism ... In

---

[26] For excerpts from the text, posted in English translation on the Arab portal al-bab ('Gateway'), see: http://www.al-bab.com/arab/docs/league/communique02.htm. (11360)

[27] Defending Palestinian suicide bombers. Kuala Lumpur, Malaysia, April 3, 2002. See: http://www.mefacts.com/cache/html/islam/11369.htm. (11369). See also "Malaysia PM: Arm Islam, Fight Jews" at: http://www.mefacts.com/cache/html/antisemitism/10514.htm (10514) and http://www.mefacts.com/cache/html/icj/11482.htm. (11482)

This document uses extensive links via the Internet. If you experience a broken link, please note the 5 digit number (xxxxx) at the end of the URL and use it as a Keyword in the Search Box at www.MEfacts.com.

effect, the Islamic conference sanctioned not only terrorism but also suicide as legitimate political instruments ... It is hard to imagine any other grouping of the world's nations that could reach such a self-destructive and morally repugnant conclusion ... Muslim spokesmen protest that terrorism is not easily defined. ... And yet it should not be hard to agree that a person who detonates himself in a pizza parlor or a discotheque filled with children, spraying scrap metal and nails in an effort to kill and maim as many of them as possible, has done something evil that can only discredit and damage whatever cause he hopes to advance."

It continued and warned prophetically:

"That Muslim governments cannot agree on this is shameful evidence of their own moral and political corruption. ... The Palestinian national cause will never recover – nor should it – until its leadership is willing to break definitively with the bombers. And Muslim states that support such sickening carnage will risk not just stigma but also their own eventual self-destruction."

The Bench of the International Court of Justice is convinced that such an organization can contribute to its deliberations.

The ICJ preferred to discount the existence of Palestinian self-rule[28] and the role of the PA and Arafat in encouraging, financing, directing and even engaging directly in terrorism.[29] It also ignored the solidarity Palestinian society has exhibited toward terrorism.

At the time of the hearings, reputable Palestinian pollster, Dr. Khalil Shikaki of Ramallah, found broad public support for terrorism and the belief that 'terrorism pays off.' In late September 2004 following the ICJ opinion that judges terrorism immaterial, Dr. Shikaki's annual poll found 77 percent of all Palestinians support the double suicide bombing

---

[28] See Main Points of Gaza-Jericho Agreement (Oslo) at: http://www.mfa.gov.il/MFA/ Peace%20Process/Guide%20to%20the%20Peace%20Process/Main%20Points%20of%2 0Gaza-Jericho%20Agremeent. (11371)

[29] See IDF report: "Arafat's and the PA's Involvement in Terrorism" at: http://www.intelli- gence.org.il/eng/bu/financing/pdfs/03.pdf. (11372)

This document uses extensive links via the Internet. If you experience a broken link, please note the 5 digit number (xxxxx) at the end of the URL and use it as a Keyword in the Search Box at www.MEfacts.com.

of two public buses in Beersheba (compared to 75 percent for a similar act at the Maxsim restaurant in Haifa in October 2003 before the issuing the ICJ's opinion); 75 percent support the shelling of Israeli civilian settlements from Gaza; and 64 percent (up from 59 percent in October 2003) "believe armed confrontations have helped Palestinians achieve their national rights in ways that negotiations could not."[30]

---

[30] See polls by pollster Dr. Khalil Shukaki, at: www.pcpsr.org.

R EPLY

2 The "Mandate for Palestine"

The "Mandate for Palestine" was conferred on April 24 1920 at the San Remo Conference and its terms outlined in the Treaty of Severs on August 10 1920. The Mandate's terms were finalized on July 24 1922 and became operational in 1923.

The Mandate laid down the Jewish right to settle anywhere in western Palestine, the area between the Jordan River and the Mediterranean Sea, an entitlement unaltered in international law and valid to this day.[31]

In paragraphs 68 and 69 of the opinion, ICJ states it will first "determine whether or not the construction of that wall breaches international law," noting that this question requires the ICJ to "make a brief analysis of the status of the territory concerned." The opinion quotes *hundreds of documents* as relevant to the case at hand, but only a few paragraphs are devoted to this fundamental question. Moreover, when it comes to discussing the significance of the 'founding document' regarding the status of the territory in question – situated between the Jordan River and the Mediterranean Sea, including the State of Israel, the West Bank and Gaza – the ICJ devotes a mere 237 words to nearly 30 years of history when Great Britain ruled the land it called Palestine. The ICJ, in noting it would briefly analyze "the status of the territory concerned," fails to cite the content of the document the "Mandate for Palestine."

---

[31] See Appendix A "Mandate for Palestine."

All the more remarkable, the ICJ *thinks* the "Mandate for Palestine" was the founding document for Arab Palestinians' self-determination!

The ICJ's narrative in paragraph 70 reads:

> "Palestine was part of the Ottoman Empire. At the end of the First World War, a class 'A' Mandate for Palestine was entrusted to Great Britain by the League of Nations, pursuant to paragraph 4 of Article 22 of the Covenant, which provided that: 'Certain communities, formerly belonging to the Turkish Empire, have reached a stage of development where their existence as independent nations can be provisionally recognized, subject to the rendering of administrative advice and assistance by a Mandatory until such time as they are able to stand alone.'"[32]

The ICJ, throughout its lengthy opinion, speaks incessantly of "Palestinians" and "Palestine" as an *Arab entity*, failing to identify these two terms and making no clarification as to the nature of the "Mandate for Palestine."

The judges also choose to speak of "Palestine" in lieu of the actual wording of the historic document that established the Mandate for Palestine – "territory of Palestine."[33] The latter would demonstrate that "Palestine" is a geographic designation, like the Great Plains, and not a polity. In fact, Palestine has never been an independent state belonging to any people, nor did a Palestinian people, distinct from other Arabs, appear during 1,300 years of Muslim hegemony in "Palestine" under Arab and Ottoman rule. Local Arabs during that rule were actually considered part of and subject to the authority of Greater Syria *(Suriyya al-Kubra)*.

---

[32] ICJ ruling, 9 July 2004, see: http://middleeastfacts.org/content/ICJ/ICJ-Ruling-HTML.htm. (10908)

[33] See Appendix A, "Mandate for Palestine," first sentence: "Whereas the Principal Allied Powers have agreed, for the purpose of giving effect to the provisions of Article 22 of the Covenant of the League of Nations, to entrust to a Mandatory selected by the said Powers the administration of the *territory of Palestine*, which formerly belonged to the Turkish Empire, within such boundaries as may be fixed by them." [italics by author]

This document uses extensive links via the Internet. If you experience a broken link, please note the 5 digit number (xxxxx) at the end of the URL and use it as a Keyword in the Search Box at www.MEfacts.com.

'Palestine' is a Geographical area, Not a Nationality

Below is a copy of the document as filed at the British National Archive, describing the delineation of the geographical area called Palestine:

PALESTINE

INTRODUCTORY.

POSITION, ETC.

Palestine lies on the western edge of the continent of Asia between Latitude 30° N. and 33° N., Longitude 34° 30' E. and 35° 30' E.

On the North it is bounded by the French Mandated Territories of Syria and Lebanon, on the East by Syria and Trans-Jordan, on the South-west by the Egyptian province of Sinai, on the South-east by the Gulf of Aqaba and on the West by the Mediterranean. The frontier with Syria was laid down by the Anglo-French Convention of the 23rd December, 1920, and its delimitation was ratified in 1923. Briefly stated, the boundaries are as follows:

North.-From Ras en Naqura on the Mediterranean eastwards to a point west of Qadas, thence in a northerly direction to Metulla, thence east to a point west of Banias.

East.-From Banias in a southerly direction east of Lake Hula to Jisr Banat Ya'pub, thence along a line east of the Jordan and the Lake of Tiberias and on to El Hamme station on the Samakh-Deraa railway line, thence along the centre of the river Yarmuq to its confluence with the Jordan, thence along the centres of the Jordan, the Dead Sea and the Wadi Araba to a point on the Gulf of Aqaba two miles west of the town of Aqaba, thence along the shore of the Gulf of Aqaba to Ras Jaba.

South.-From Ras Jaba in a generally north-westerly direction to the junction of the Neki-Aqaba and Gaza Aqaba Roads, thence to a point west-north-west of Ain Maghara and thence to a point on the Mediterranean coast north-west of Rafa.

West.-The Mediterranean Sea.

Like a mantra, Arabs, the UN, its organs and now the International Court of Justice have claimed repeatedly that the Palestinians are a native people – so much so that almost everyone takes it for granted. The problem is that a stateless Palestinian people is a fabrication. The word 'Palestine' is not even Arabic.[34]

---

[34] For more on this subject see, Popular Searches: Territories and Palestinians at http://www. MEfacts.com.

In a report by His Majesty's Government in the United Kingdom of Great Britain and Northern Ireland to the Council of the League of Nations on the administration of Palestine and Trans-Jordan for the year 1938, the British made it clear: *Palestine is not a State but is the name of a geographical area.*[35]

The ICJ Bench creates the impression that the League of Nations was speaking of a nascent state or national grouping – the Palestinians who were one of the 'communities' mentioned in Article 22 of the League of Nations. *Nothing could be farther from the truth.* The Mandate for Palestine was a Mandate for Jewish self-determination.

Either the learned judges chose to deliberately mislead the public, or they were totally unaware of the content of this most significant legally-binding document regarding the status of the Territories.

Paragraph 1 of Article 22 of the Covenant of the League of Nations reads:

> "To those colonies and territories which as a consequence of the late war have ceased to be under the sovereignty of the States which formerly governed them and which are inhabited by peoples not yet able to stand by themselves under the strenuous conditions of the modern world, there should be applied

---

[35] Palestine is a word coined by the Romans around 135 CE from the name of a seagoing Aegean people who settled on the coast of Canaan in antiquity – the Philistines. The name was chosen to replace Judea, as a sign that Jewish sovereignty had been eradicated after the Jewish Revolt against Rome. In the course of time, the name Philistia in Latin was further bastardized into Palistina or Palestine. In modern times the name 'Palestine' or 'Palestinian' was applied as an adjective to all inhabitants of the geographical area between the Mediterranean Sea and the Jordan River – Palestinian Jews and Palestinian Arabs alike. In fact, up until the 1960s, most Arabs in Palestine preferred to identify themselves merely as part of the great Arab nation or as part of Arab Syria.

Until recently, no Arab nation or group recognized or claimed the existence of an independent Palestinian nationality or ethnicity. Arabs who happened to live in Palestine denied that they had a unique Palestinian identity. The First Congress of Muslim-Christian Associations (Jerusalem, February 1919) met to select Palestinian Arab representatives for the Paris Peace Conference. They adopted the following resolution: "We consider Palestine as part of Arab Syria, as it has never been separated from it at any time. We are connected with it by national, religious, linguistic, natural, economic and geographical bonds." See Yehoshua Porath, "The Palestinian Arab National Movement: From Riots to Rebellion," Frank Cass and Co., Ltd, London, 1977, vol. 2, pp. 81-82.

the principle that the well-being and development of such peoples form a sacred trust of civilization and that securities for the performance of this trust should be embodied in this Covenant."[36]

The Palestinian Royal Commission Report of July, 1937 addresses Arab claims that the creation of the Jewish National Home as directed by the Mandate for Palestine violated Article 22 of the Covenant of the League of Nations:

"As to the claim, argued before us by Arab witnesses, that the Palestine Mandate violates Article 22 of the Covenant because it is not in accordance with paragraph 4 thereof, we would point out (a) that the provisional recognition of 'certain communities formerly belonging to the Turkish Empire' as independent nations is permissive; the words are '*can* be provisionally recognised', not 'will' or '*shall*': (b) that the penultimate paragraph of Article 22 prescribes that the degree of authority to be exercised by the Mandatory shall be defined, at need, by the Council of the League: (c) that the acceptance by the Allied Powers and the United States of the policy of the Balfour Declaration made it clear from the beginning that Palestine would have to be treated differently from Syria and Iraq, and that this difference of treatment was confirmed by the Supreme Council in the Treaty of Sevres and by the Council of the League in sanctioning the Mandate. [E.H. The "Mandate for Palestine" was conferred on April 24, 1920 at the San Remo Conference and its terms were delineated on August 10, 1920 in Article 95 of the Treaty of Severs. The Mandate's document was finalized on July 24 1922.]

"This particular question is of less practical importance than it might seem to be. For Article 2 of the Mandate requires 'the development of self-governing institutions'; and, read in the light of the general intention of the Mandate System (of which something will be said presently), this requirement implies, in our judgment, the ultimate establishment of independence.

"(3) The field [Territory] in which the Jewish National Home was to be established was understood, at the time of the Balfour Declaration, to be the whole of historic Palestine, and the Zionists were seriously disappointed when Trans-Jordan was cut away from that field [Territory] under Article 25."[37] (E.H. That excluded 76 percent of the original area – east of the Jordan River, what became later Trans-Jordan.)

---

[36] Article 22 of The Covenant of The League of Nations, A/297, 30 April 1947 at: http://middleeastfacts.org/content/UN-Documents/A-297-30-April-1947-conenant-article-22.htm. (10925)

[37] Palestine Royal Report, July 1937, Chapter II, p. 38.

This document uses extensive links via the Internet. If you experience a broken link, please note the 5 digit number (xxxxx) at the end of the URL and use it as a Keyword in the Search Box at www.MEfacts.com.

The "inhabitants" of the territory for whom the Mandate for Palestine was created, who according to the Mandate were "not yet able" to govern themselves and for whom self-determination was a "sacred trust," were not Palestinians, or even Arabs. The Mandate for Palestine was created by the predecessor of the United Nations, the League of Nations, for the *Jewish People.*[38]

The second paragraph of the preamble of the Mandate for Palestine therefore reads:

"Whereas the Principal Allied Powers have also agreed that the Mandatory should be responsible for putting into effect the declaration originally made on November 2nd, 1917, by the Government of His Britannic Majesty, and adopted by the said Powers, in favor of the *establishment in Palestine of a national home for the Jewish people,* it being clearly understood that nothing should be done which might prejudice the civil and religious rights of existing non-Jewish communities in Palestine ... *Recognition has thereby been given to the historical connection of the Jewish people with Palestine and to the grounds for reconstituting their national home in that country ...*"[39] [italics by author].

Addressing the Arab claim that Palestine was part of the territories promised to the Arabs in 1915 by Sir Henry McMahon, the British Government stated:

"We think it sufficient for the purposes of this Report to state that the British Government have *never accepted the Arab case.* When it was first formally presented by the Arab Delegation in London in 1922, the Secretary of State for the Colonies (Mr. Churchill) replied as follows:

"That letter [Sir H. McMahon's letter of the 24th October, 1915] is quoted as conveying the promise to the Sherif of Mecca to recognize and support the independence of the Arabs within the territories proposed by him. But this promise was given subject to a reservation made in the same letter, which excluded from its scope, among other territories, the portions of Syria lying to the west of the district of Damascus. This reservation has always been regarded by His Majesty's Government as covering the vilayet of Beirut and the independent Sanjak of Jerusalem. *The whole of Palestine west of the Jordan was thus excluded from Sir H. McMahon's pledge.*

---

[38] See: Appendix A "Mandate for Palestine."
[39] Ibid.

"It was in the highest degree unfortunate that, in the exigencies of war, the British Government was unable to make their intention clear to the Sherif. *Palestine*, it will have been noticed, *was not expressly mentioned* in Sir Henry McMahon's letter of the 24th October, 1915. Nor was any later reference made to it. In the further correspondence between Sir Henry McMahon and the Sherif the only areas relevant to the present discussion which were mentioned were the Vilayets of Aleppo and Beirut. The Sherif asserted that these Vilayets were purely Arab; and, when Sir Henry McMahon pointed out that French interests were involved, he replied that, while he did not recede from his full claims in the north, he did not wish to injure the alliance between Britain and France and would not ask 'for what we now leave to France in Beirut and its coasts' till after the War. There was no more bargaining over boundaries. It only remained for the British Government to supply the Sherif with the monthly subsidy in gold and the rifles, ammunition and foodstuffs he required for launching and sustaining the revolt."[40] [italics by author].

In recent decades, Palestinians have been quite successful in co-opting for themselves the term 'Palestinian'. It appears that the author of the opinion, the President of the ICJ, was totally unaware of the fact that "Palestinian" was once a 'Jewish' term, a phenomenon to be discussed elsewhere in this critique.

A 'Classless' "Mandate for Palestine"

The Court's president also assumed that the "Mandate for Palestine" was a Class "A" mandate,[41] a common, but inaccurate assertion that can be found in many dictionaries and encyclopedias, and is frequently used by the pro-Palestinian media. In paragraph 70 of the opinion, the Court erroneously states that:

"Palestine was part of the Ottoman Empire. At the end of the First World War, *a class [type] 'A' Mandate for Palestine* was entrusted to Great Britain by the League of Nations, pursuant to paragraph 4 of Article 22 of the Covenant ..."[42] [italics by author]

---

[40] The "Palestine Royal Report," July 1937, Chapter II, p. 20.

[41] ICJ uses the term 'Class A' while the British Government used the term 'Special Regime.'

[42] ICJ ruling, 9 July 2004, see: http://middleeastfacts.org/content/ICJ/ICJ-Ruling-HTML.htm. (10908)

This document uses extensive links via the Internet. If you experience a broken link, please note the 5 digit number (xxxxx) at the end of the URL and use it as a Keyword in the Search Box at www.MEfacts.com.

Indeed, Class "A" status was granted to a number of Arab peoples who were ready for independence in the former Ottoman Empire, and only to Arab entities.[43] Palestinian Arabs were not one of these 'Arab peoples.' The Palestine Royal Report clarifies this point:

> "(2) The Mandate [for Palestine] is of a *different type* from the Mandate for Syria and the Lebanon and the draft Mandate for Iraq [E.H. and later Trans-Jordan]. These latter, which were called for convenience "A" Mandates, accorded with the fourth paragraph of Article 22. Thus the Syrian Mandate provided that the government should be based on an organic law which should take into account the rights, interests and wishes of all the inhabitants, and that measures should be enacted "to facilitate the progressive development of Syria and the Lebanon as independent States". The corresponding sentences of the draft Mandate for `Iraq were the same. In compliance with them National Legislatures were established in due course on an elective basis. Article 1 of the *Palestine Mandate, on the other hand,* vests "full powers of legislation and of administration", within the limits of the Mandate, in the Mandatory."[44, 45] [italics by author]

The Palestine Royal Report highlight additional differences:

> "Unquestionably, however, the primary purpose of the Mandate, as expressed in its preamble and its articles, is to promote the establishment of the Jewish National Home.

> "(5) Articles 4, 6 and 11 provide for the recognition of a Jewish Agency 'as a public body for the purpose of advising and co-operating with the Administration' on matters affecting Jewish interests. No such body is envisaged for dealing with Arab interests.[46]

---

[43] Class "A" mandates assigned to Britain were Iraq and Transjordan. Assigned to France were Syria and Lebanon. Examples of other type of Mandates were the Class "B" mandate assigned to Belgium administrating Ruanda-Urundi, and the Class "C" mandate assigned to South Africa administering South West Africa.

[44] The "Palestine Royal Report", July 1937, Chapter II, p.38.

[45] Claims that Palestinian self-determination was granted under Chapter 22 of the UN Charter and the 'pre-existence' of an Arab governmental structure (of a host of fallacies) can be found in Issa Nakhlah, "Encyclopedia of the Palestinian Problem" at http://www.palestine-encyclopedia.com/EPP/Chapter01.htm. (11452)

[46] Palestine Royal Report, July 1937, Chapter II, p. 39.

This document uses extensive links via the Internet. If you experience a broken link, please note the 5 digit number (xxxxx) at the end of the URL and use it as a Keyword in the Search Box at www.MEfacts.com.

"48. But Palestine was *different* from the other ex-Turkish provinces. It was, indeed, *unique* both as the Holy Land of three world-religions and as the old historic homeland of the Jews. The Arabs had lived in it for centuries, but they had long ceased to rule it, and in view of its peculiar character they could not now claim to possess it in the same way as they could claim possession of Syria or 'Iraq'."[47] [italics by author].

Why was identifying the Mandate for Palestine as Class "A" important to the ICJ?

There is much to be gained by attributing Class "A" status to the Mandate for Palestine. If 'the inhabitants of Palestine' were ready for independence under a Class "A" mandate, then the Palestinian Arabs that made up the majority of the inhabitants of Palestine in 1922 (589,177 Arabs vs. 83,790 Jews),[48] could then logically claim that they were the intended beneficiaries of the Mandate for Palestine – provided one never reads the actual wording of the document:

1. The "Mandate for Palestine"[49] *never mentions Class "A" status at any time* for Palestinian Arabs.

2. Article 2 clearly speaks of the Mandatory as being

> "responsible for placing the country under such political, administrative and economic conditions as will secure the establishment of the *Jewish national home*," [italics by author]

The Mandate calls for steps to encourage *Jewish immigration and settlement* throughout Palestine except east of the Jordan River. Historically, therefore, Palestine was an 'anomaly' within the Mandate system, 'in a class of its own' – initially referred by the British as a "special regime."[50]

---

47 Ibid. p. 40.
48 Citing by the UN. 1922 Census. See at: http://www.unu.edu/unupress/unupbooks/ 80859e/80859E05.htm. (11373)
49 See: Appendix A "Mandate for Palestine."
50 Palestine Royal Report, July 1937, Chapter II, p. 28, paragraph 29.

This document uses extensive links via the Internet. If you experience a broken link, please note the 5 digit number (xxxxx) at the end of the URL and use it as a Keyword in the Search Box at www.MEfacts.com.

It seems that the ICJ simply took false Arab claims at face value, without examining the evidence.

Had the ICJ Bench examined all six pages of the Mandate of Palestine document, it would have noted that several times the Mandate for Palestine clearly differentiates between *political* rights – referring to Jewish self-determination as an emerging polity and *civil* rights – referring to guarantees of equal personal freedoms to non-Jewish residents as individuals and within select communities. Not once are Arabs as a people mentioned in the Mandate for Palestine. At no point in the entire document is there any granting of political rights to non-Jewish entities (i.e. Arabs) because political rights to self-determination as a polity for Arabs were guaranteed in four other parallel Class "A" mandates – in Lebanon, Syria, Iraq, and later, Trans-Jordan. Again, the Bench chose to either ignore these facts or failed to do its history homework. For instance, Article 2 of the Mandate states explicitly that the Mandatory should:

> "... be responsible for placing the country under such *political*, administrative and economic conditions as will secure the establishment of the *Jewish national home*, as laid down in the preamble, and the development of self-governing institutions, and also for safeguarding the *civil* and religious *rights* of all the inhabitants of Palestine, irrespective of race and religion." [italics by author]

Eleven times in the Mandate for Palestine, the League of Nations speaks specifically of Jews and the Jewish people, calling upon Great Britain to create a nationality law

> "to facilitate the acquisition of Palestinian citizenship by Jews who take up their permanent residence in Palestine,"

There is not one mention of the word "Palestinians" or the phrase "Palestinian Arabs," as it is exploited today. Alas, the "non-Jewish communities" the Mandate speaks of were extensions (or in today's parlance, 'diaspora communities') of another Arab people for whom a *separate* mandate had been drawn up at the same time – the Syrians that the International Court of Justice ignored in its so-called 'discussion' of the Mandate system.[51] It is important to note that not only Britain and France were Mandators (e.g. official administrators and mentors), but also Belgium, New Zealand, South Africa, and Japan elsewhere – mandates that created Cameroon, Rwanda, Samoa and New Guinea (today's Papua New Guinea).

Consequently, it is not surprising that a local Arab leader, Auni Bey Abdul-Hadi, stated in his testimony in 1937 before the Peel Commission:

> "There is no such country [as Palestine]! Palestine is a term the Zionists invented! There is no Palestine in the Bible. Our country was for centuries, part of Syria."[52]

But the ICJ remained unaware that the term 'Palestinian' had only been invented in the 1960s to paint Jews – who had adopted the term 'Israelis' after the establishment of the State of Israel – as invaders now residing on Arab turf. The ICJ was unaware that written into the terms of the Mandate, Palestinian Jews had been directed to establish a Jewish Agency for Palestine to further Jewish settlements (today, the Jewish Agency), or that since 1902 there had been an Anglo-Palestine Bank, established by the Zionist Movement (today Bank Leumi). Nor did they know that Jews had established a Palestine Philharmonic Orchestra in 1936 (today, the Israeli Philharmonic) and an English-language newspaper called the *Palestine Post* in 1932 (today named the *Jerusalem Post*) – along with numerous other Jewish 'Palestinian institutions.'

Consequently, the ICJ incorrectly cites the 'unfulfilled Mandate for Palestine' as justification for the Bench's intervention in the case – assuming or willfully making it appear there was supposed to be a fifth Arab Mandate – Palestine. The ICJ argues that as the judicial arm of the

---

[51] For a brief description of the Mandate System, see Q. Wright, *Mandates under the League of Nations* (1930, Repr. 1968) cited on Fact Monster, at: http://www.factmonster.com/ce6/history/A0831495.html.

[52] For this and a host of other quotes from Arab spokespersons on the Syrian identity of local Arabs, see http://www.yahoodi.com/peace/palestinians.html.

United Nations, the International Court of Justice has jurisdiction in this case because of its responsibility as a UN institution for bringing Palestinian self-determination to fruition! In paragraph 49 of the opinion, the Bench declares, mistakenly, that:

> "… the Court does not consider that the subject-matter of the General Assembly's request can be regarded as only a bilateral matter between Israel and Palestine …[therefore] construction of the wall must be deemed to be directly of concern to the United Nations. The responsibility of the United Nations in this matter also has its *origin in the Mandate* and the Partition Resolution concerning Palestine.[53] This responsibility has been described by the General Assembly as 'a permanent responsibility towards the question of Palestine until the question is resolved in all its aspects in a satisfactory manner in accordance with international legitimacy' (General Assembly resolution 57/107 of 3 December 2002.) …" the objective being "the realization of the inalienable rights of the Palestinian people." [italics by author]

To the average reader lacking a profound historical knowledge of this conflict, the term 'Mandate for Palestine,' sound like an Arab trusteeship, but this interpretation changes neither history nor legal facts about Israel.

Had the ICJ examined the minutes of the report of the 1947 United Nations Special Committee on Palestine,[54] among the myriad of documents it did 'examine,' the learned judges would have known that the Arabs categorically rejected the Mandate for Palestine. In the July 22, 1947 testimony of the President of the Council of Lebanon, Hamid Frangie, the Lebanese Minister of Foreign Affairs, speaking on behalf of all the Arab countries, declared unequivocally:

> "There is only one solution for the Palestinian problem, namely cessation of the Mandate [for the Jews]" and both the Balfour Declaration and the Mandate are "null and valueless." All of Palestine, he claimed, "is in fact an integral part of this Arab world, which is organized into sovereign States

---

[53] See paragraphs 70 and 71 of the ICJ ruling, 9 July 2004, see: http://middleeastfacts.org/content/ICJ/ICJ-Ruling-HTML.htm. (10908)

[54] See document at: http://www.mefacts.com/cache/html/un-documents/11188.htm. (11188)

This document uses extensive links via the Internet. If you experience a broken link, please note the 5 digit number (xxxxx) at the end of the URL and use it as a Keyword in the Search Box at www.MEfacts.com.

bound together by the political and economic pact of 22 March 1945"[55] [E.H. the Arab League] – with no mention of an Arab Palestinian state.

Frangie warned of more bloodshed:

> "The Governments of the Arab States will not under any circumstances agree to permit the establishment of Zionism as an autonomous State on Arab territory" and that Arab countries "wish to state that they feel certain that the partition of Palestine and the creation of a Jewish State would result only in *bloodshed* and unrest throughout the entire Middle East."[56] [italics by author]

This is not the only document that would have instructed the judges that the Mandate for Palestine was not for Arab Palestinians. Article 20[57] of the PLO Charter, adopted by the Palestine National Council in July 1968 and never legally revised,[58] and proudly posted on the Palestinian delegation's UN website, states:

> "The Balfour Declaration, the Mandate for Palestine, and everything that has been based upon them, are deemed null and void."[59]

The PLO Charter adds that Jews do not meet the criteria of a nationality and therefore do not deserve statehood at all, clarifying this statement in Article 21 of the Palestinian Charter, that Palestinians,

> "... reject all solutions which are substitutes for the total liberation of Palestine."

---

[55] Ibid.

[56] Ibid.

[57] Article 20 of the PLO Charter: "The Balfour Declaration, the Mandate for Palestine, and everything that has been based upon them, are deemed null and void. Claims of historical or religious ties of Jews with Palestine are incompatible with the facts of history and the true conception of what constitutes statehood. Judaism, being a religion, is not an independent nationality. Nor do Jews constitute a single nation with an identity of its own; they are citizens of the states to which they belong." (10366)

[58] The Palestinians pretend that all anti-Israel clauses were abolished in a three day meeting of the Palestinian National Council in Gaza in April 1996. In fact, the Council took only a bureaucratic decision to establish a committee to discuss abolishment of the clauses that call for the destruction of Israel as they had promised to do at the outset of the Oslo Accords, and no further action has been taken by this 'committee' to this day.

[59] See Permanent Missions to the UN, at: http://www.palestine-un.org/plo/pna_three.html. (11361)

This document uses extensive links via the Internet. If you experience a broken link, please note the 5 digit number (xxxxx) at the end of the URL and use it as a Keyword in the Search Box at www.MEfacts.com.

It is difficult to ignore yet another instance of historical fantasy, where the ICJ also quotes extensively from Article 13 of the Mandate for Palestine with respect to Jerusalem's Holy Places and access to them as one of the foundations for Palestinian rights allegedly violated by the security barrier (along with quotes from other documents). The ICJ states in paragraph 129 of the Opinion:

> "In addition to the general guarantees of freedom of movement under Article 12 of the International Covenant on Civil and Political Rights, account must also be taken of specific guarantees of access to the Christian, Jewish and Islamic Holy Places. The status of the Christian Holy Places in the Ottoman Empire dates far back in time, the latest provisions relating thereto having been incorporated into Article 62 of the Treaty of Berlin of 13 July 1878. The Mandate for Palestine given to the British Government on 24 July 1922 included an Article 13, under which:

> "All responsibility in connection with the Holy Places and religious buildings or sites in Palestine, including that of preserving existing rights and of securing free access to the Holy Places, religious buildings and sites and the free exercise of worship, while ensuring the requirements of public order and decorum, is assumed by the Mandatory ..." Article 13 further stated: - "nothing in this mandate shall be construed as conferring ... authority to interfere with the fabric or the management of purely Moslem sacred shrines, the immunities of which are guaranteed."[60]

In fact, the 187 word quote is longer than the ICJ's entire treatment of nearly three decades of British Mandate, which is summed up in one sentence, and is part of the ICJ 'rewriting' of history:

> "In 1947 the United Kingdom announced its intention to complete evacuation of the mandated territory by 1 August 1948, subsequently advancing that date to 15 May 1948."[61]

The Preamble of the Mandate for Palestine as well as the other 28 articles of this legal document, including eight articles of which specifically refer

---

[60] ICJ ruling, 9 July 2004, see: http://middleeastfacts.org/content/ICJ/ICJ-Ruling-HTML.htm. (10908)

[61] Ibid. Paragraph 71.

This document uses extensive links via the Internet. If you experience a broken link, please note the 5 digit number (xxxxx) at the end of the URL and use it as a Keyword in the Search Box at www.MEfacts.com.

to the *Jewish* nature of the Mandate and discuss where Jews are legally permitted to settle and where they are not, *appear nowhere* in the Court's document.[62]

The origin of the "Mandate for Palestine" the ICJ overlooked – started in 1920

The "Mandate for Palestine" was conferred on April 24, 1920 at the San Remo Conference, and the terms of the Mandate were further delineated on August 10, 1920. Article 95 of the Treaty of Sevres reads:

> "The High Contracting Parties agree to entrust, by application of the provisions of Article 22, the administration of Palestine, within such boundaries as may be determined by the Principal Allied Powers, to a Mandatory to be selected by the said Powers. The Mandatory will be responsible for putting into effect the declaration originally made on November 2, 1917, by the British Government, and adopted by the other Allied Powers, in favour of the establishment in Palestine of a national home for the Jewish people ..." [E.H. The Mandate for Palestine document was finalized and signed on July 24, 1922, and became operational in 1923]

Articles 94 and 95 of the Treaty of Sevres, which the ICJ never discussed, completely undermines the ICJ's argument that the Mandate for Palestine was a Class "A" Mandate. This erroneous claim by the International Court of Justice, renders the Court's subsequent assertions baseless. The Bench has shown a total misunderstanding of the applicable international law.

---

[62] See: Appendix A, Article 2 of the "Mandate for Palestine."

"The Mandatory shall be responsible for placing the country under such political, administrative and economic conditions as will secure the establishment of the Jewish national home, as laid down in the preamble, and the development of self-governing institutions, and also for safeguarding the civil and religious rights of all the inhabitants of Palestine, irrespective of race and religion."

The "Mandate for Palestine" – Protected by Article 80 of the UN Charter

In paragraph 162 of the Advisory Opinion, the Court states:

> "Since 1947, the year when General Assembly resolution 181 (II) was adopted and the *Mandate for Palestine was terminated,* there has been a succession of armed conflicts, acts of indiscriminate violence and repressive measures on the former mandated territory." [italics by author]

The Court attempts to 'overcome' historical legal facts by making the reader believe that adoption of Resolution 181 by the General Assembly in 1947 – a resolution that all Arab States voted against as a bloc and whose implementation they promised to defy – and indeed did so by use of force, has presently legal standing. In fact, Resolution 181 was a non-binding *recommendation,* whose implementation hinged on acceptance by *both* parties, yet the ICJ views it as if it was a binding directive with the power to amend the above-mentioned international accords, irrespective of its acceptance by the parties (See Chapter 4, "Resolution 181 – The Partition Plan").

The Court is also in the wrong when it states that the "Mandate for Palestine was terminated" – with no substantiation as to how this could take place, since the Mandates of the League of Nations have a special status in international law and are considered to be 'sacred trusts.' A trust – as in Article 80 of the UN Charter – does not end because the trustee fades away. The Mandate for Palestine, an international accord that was never amended, survived the British withdrawal in 1948, and is a binding legal instrument, valid to this day (See Chapter 10: "Territories – Legality of Jewish Settlement").

This grave blunder by the International Court of Justice compelled the author to enclose, as end pages of this critique in Appendix A, a full copy of the document, "Mandate for Palestine."

3 Jerusalem and the Holy Places

The ICJ completely ignores the fact that Palestinians turned the City of Peace into their primary target for suicide bombers, making a barrier to impede movement of terrorists into the heart of the city an imperative.

Judge, Sir Elihu Lauterpacht on the City of Peace:

"Jerusalem, it seems, is at the physical center of the Arab-Israeli conflict. In fact, two distinct issues exist: the issue of Jerusalem and the issue of the Holy Places.

Not only are the two problems separate; they are also quite distinct in nature from one another. So far as the Holy Places are concerned, the question is for the most part one of assuring respect for the existing interests of the three religions and of providing the necessary guarantees of freedom of access, worship, and religious administration. Questions of this nature are only marginally an issue between Israel and her neighbors and their solution should not complicate the peace negotiations. As far as the City of Jerusalem itself is concerned, the question is one of establishing an effective administration of the City which can protect the rights of the various elements of its permanent population – Christian, Arab and Jewish – and ensure the governmental stability and physical security which are essential requirements for the city of the Holy Places."[63]

---

[63] Professor, Judge, Sir Elihu Lauterpacht, "Jerusalem and the Holy Places," Pamphlet No. 19 (London, Anglo-Israel Association, 1968). Professor Elihu Lauterpacht, is a highly experienced academic and practitioner in the field of public international law. He has been active as an international litigator, advisor and arbitrator. Among the countries for which he has appeared in land and maritime boundary cases are Bahrain, Chile, El Salvador, Israel, Malta and Namibia. He is an ad hoc Judge of the International Court of Justice, and has been an arbitrator in a number of cases in the International Centre for the Settlement of Investment Disputes and in various other international cases. He is an honorary Professor of the University of Cambridge where he taught for thirty five years, and is the founder and first Director of the Research Centre for International Law.

The ICJ Fixation - Internationalization of Jerusalem

> "Nothing was said in the Mandate about the internationalization of Jerusalem. Indeed Jerusalem as such is not mentioned, – though the Holy Places are. And this in itself is a fact of relevance now. For it shows that in 1922 there was no inclination to identify the question of the Holy Places with that of the internationalization of Jerusalem."[64]

Arab leaders, including Palestinians, now supported by this ICJ opinion have sought to justify their right to Jerusalem by distorting the meaning of United Nations resolutions which apply to the city. UN General Assembly Resolution 181 *recommended* turning Jerusalem and its environs into an international city, or corpus separatum. Again, Arab spokesmen conveniently ignore the fact that Resolution 181 was a *non-binding recommendation* that was never consummated.

Professor Julius Stone notes that Resolution 181 "lacked binding force" from the outset, since it required acceptance by all parties concerned:

> "While the state of Israel did for her part express willingness to accept it, the other states concerned both rejected it and took up arms unlawfully against it."[65]

Judge, Sir Elihu Lauterpacht wrote in 1968, just one year after the 1967 Six-Day War, about the new conditions that had arisen since 1948 with regard to the original thoughts of the internationalization of Jerusalem:

> - "The Arab States rejected the Partition Plan and the proposal for the internationalization of Jerusalem.

> - "The Arab States physically opposed the implementation of the General Assembly Resolution. They sought by force of arms to expel the Jewish inhabitants of Jerusalem and to achieve sole occupation of the City.

---

[64] Ibid.

[65] Professor Julius Stone (1907-1985), "Israel and Palestine, Assault on the Law of Nations" *The Johns Hopkins University Press,* 1981, p. 127. The late Professor Julius Stone was recognized as one of the twentieth century's leading authorities on the Law of Nations. His work represents a detailed analysis of the central principles of international law governing the issues raised by the Arab-Israel conflict. He was one of a few scholars to gain outstanding recognition in more than one field. Professor Stone was one of the world's best-known authorities in both Jurisprudence and International Law.

- "In the event, Jordan obtained control only of the Eastern part of the City, including the Walled City.

- "While Jordan permitted reasonably free access to Christian Holy Places, it denied the Jews any access to the Jewish Holy Places. This was a fundamental departure from the tradition of freedom of religious worship in the Holy Land, which had evolved over centuries. It was also a clear violation of the undertaking given by Jordan in the Armistice Agreement concluded with Israel on 3rd April, 1949. Article VIII of this Agreement called for the establishment of a Special Committee of Israeli and Jordanian representatives to formulate agreed plans on certain matters which, in any case, shall include the following, on which agreement in principle already exists ... free access to the Holy Places and cultural institutions and use of the Cemetery on the Mount of Olives.

- "The U.N. displayed no concern over the discrimination thus practiced against persons of the Jewish faith.

- "The U.N. accepted as tolerable the unsupervised control of the Old City of Jerusalem by Jordanian forces - notwithstanding the fact that the presence of Jordanian forces west of the Jordan River was entirely lacking in any legal justification.

- "During the period 1948-1952 the General Assembly gradually came to accept that the plan for the territorial internationalization of Jerusalem had been quite overtaken by events. From 1952 to the present time [1968] virtually nothing more has been heard of the idea in the General Assembly.

"On 5th June, 1967, Jordan deliberately overthrew the Armistice Agreement by attacking the Israeli-held part of Jerusalem. There was no question of this Jordanian action being a reaction to any Israeli attack. It took place notwithstanding explicit Israeli assurances, conveyed to King Hussein through the U.N. Commander, that if Jordan did not attack Israel, Israel would not attack Jordan. Although the charge of aggression is freely made against Israel in relation to the Six-Days War the fact remains that the two attempts made in the General Assembly in June-July 1967 to secure the condemnation of Israel as an aggressor failed. A clear and striking majority of the members of the U.N. voted against the proposition that Israel was an aggressor."[66]

---

[66] Professor, Judge, Sir Elihu Lauterpacht, "Jerusalem and the Holy Places," Pamphlet No. 19 (London, Anglo-Israel Association, 1968).

Today, more than 55 years later, Israel has reunited Jerusalem and provided unrestricted freedom of religion, with access to the Holy Places in the unified City of Peace assured.

Significant events appear to have escaped the ICJ, which mentioned Jerusalem 54 times in its opinion:

> "Moslems have enjoyed, under Israeli control, the very freedom which Jews were denied during Jordanian occupation."[67]

The UN and Jerusalem - Both the General Assembly and the Security Council have limited influence on the future of Jerusalem.

Judge, Sir Lauterpacht explains:

> "(i) The role of the U.N. in relation to the future of Jerusalem and the Holy Places is limited. In particular, the General Assembly has no power of disposition over Jerusalem and no right to lay down regulations for the Holy Places. The Security Council, of course, retains its powers under Chapter VII of the Charter in relation to threats to the peace, breaches of the peace and acts of aggression, but these powers do not extend to the adoption of any general position regarding the future of Jerusalem and the Holy Places.

> "(ii) Israel's governmental measures in relation to Jerusalem – both New and Old – are lawful and valid."

Originally, internationalization of Jerusalem was part of a much broader proposal that the Arab states rejected (Resolution 181), both at the UN and 'on the ground' – Arab's rejection by armed invasion of Palestine by the forces of Egypt, Transjordan, Syria, Lebanon, Iraq, and contingents from Saudi Arabia and Yemen … aimed at destroying Israel.

---

[67] Ibid.

The outcome of 'consistent' Arab aggression was best described by Judge Stephen Schwebel:

> "... as between Israel, acting defensively in 1948 and 1967, on the one hand, and her Arab neighbors, acting aggressively in 1948 and 1967, on the other, Israel has better title in the territory of what was Palestine, including *the whole of Jerusalem* ..."[68] [italics by author]

The historical Myth of 'Two Jerusalems,' an Arab 'East Jerusalem' and a Jewish 'West Jerusalem.'

Jerusalem was *never* an Arab city; Jews have held a majority in Jerusalem since 1870,[69] and 'east-west' is a geographic, not a political designation. It is no different than claiming the Eastern Shore of Maryland in the U.S., should be a separate political entity from the rest of that state.

Although uniting the city transformed *all* of Jerusalem into the largest city in Israel and a bustling metropolis, even moderate Palestinian leaders reject the idea of a united city. Their minimal demand for 'just East Jerusalem' really means the Jewish holy sites (including the Jewish Quarter and the Western Wall), which Arabs have historically failed to protect, and transfer to Arabs of neighborhoods that house a significant percentage of Jerusalem's present-day Jewish population. Most of that city is built on rock-strewn empty land *around* the city that was in the

---

[68] Professor, Judge Stephen M. Schwebel, *What Weight to Conquest?* in "Justice in International Law", Cambridge University Press, 1994. Judge Schwebel has served on the International Court since 15 January 1981. He was Vice-President of the Court from 1994 to 1997 and has been President from 1997 to 2000. A former Deputy Legal Adviser of the United States Department of State and Burling Professor of International Law at the School of Advanced International Studies of The Johns Hopkins University (Washington). Judge Schwebel is the author of several books and over 150 articles on international law. He is Honorary President of the American Society of International Law.

Opinions quoted in this critiques are not derived from his position as a judge of the ICJ.

[69] For these and more statistics, see "Jerusalem: The City's Development from a Historical Viewpoint," at: http://www.mfa.gov.il/MFA/MFAArchive/1990_1999/1998/7/Jerusalem-%20The%20City-s%20Development%20from%20a%20Historica. (10748)

This document uses extensive links via the Internet. If you experience a broken link, please note the 5 digit number (xxxxx) at the end of the URL and use it as a Keyword in the Search Box at www.MEfacts.com.

41

public domain for the past 36 years. With an overall population of 591,400 today, separating East Jerusalem and West Jerusalem is as viable and acceptable as the notion of splitting Berlin into two cities again, or separating East Harlem from the rest of Manhattan within New York City.

Jerusalem's Jewish Link: Historic, Religious, Political.

Jerusalem, wrote historian Martin Gilbert,[70] is not a "'mere' capital: It holds the central spiritual and physical place in the history of the Jews as a people."[71]

For more than 3,000 years, the Jewish people have looked to Jerusalem as their spiritual, political, and historical capital, even when they did not physically rule over the city. Throughout its long history, Jerusalem has served, and still serves, as the political capital of only one nation – the one belonging to the Jews. Its prominence in Jewish history began in 1004 BCE, when King David declared the city the capital of the first Jewish kingdom.[72] David's successor and son, King Solomon, built the First Temple there, according to the Bible, as a holy place to worship the Almighty. Unfortunately, history would not be kind to the Jewish people. Four hundred ten years after King Solomon completed construction of Jerusalem, the Babylonians (early ancestors to today's Iraqis) seized and destroyed the city, forcing the Jews into exile. Fifty years later, the Jews, or Israelites as they were called, were permitted to return after Persia (present-day Iran) conquered Babylon. The Jews' first order of business was to reclaim Jerusalem as their capital and rebuild the Holy Temple, recorded in history as the Second Temple.

---

[70] Martin Gilbert is an Honorary Fellow of Merton College Oxford and the biographer of Winston Churchill. He is the author of the "Jerusalem: Illustrated History Atlas" (Vallentine Mitchell) and "Jerusalem: Rebirth of the City" (Viking-Penguin).

[71] Martin Gilbert, "Jerusalem: A Tale of One City," *The New Republic,* Nov. 14, 1994. See: http://web.idirect.com/~cic/jerusalem/martinGilbertArticle.htm. (11362)

[72] Ibid.

This document uses extensive links via the Internet. If you experience a broken link, please note the 5 digit number (xxxxx) at the end of the URL and use it as a Keyword in the Search Box at www.MEfacts.com.

Jerusalem was more than the Jewish kingdom's political capital. It was a spiritual beacon. During the First and Second Temple periods, Jews throughout the kingdom would travel to Jerusalem three times yearly for the pilgrimages of the Jewish holy days of Sukkot, Passover, and Shavuot, until the Roman Empire destroyed the Second Temple in 70 CE and ended Jewish sovereignty over Jerusalem for the next 1,900 years. Despite that fate, Jews never relinquished their bond to Jerusalem or, for that matter, to *Eretz Yisrael*, the Land of Israel.

No matter where Jews lived throughout the world for those two millennia, their thoughts and prayers were directed toward Jerusalem. Even today, whether in Israel, the United States or anywhere else, Jewish ritual practice, holiday celebration and lifecycle events include recognition of Jerusalem as a core element of the Jewish experience. Consider that:

- Jews in prayer always turn toward Jerusalem.

- Arks (the sacred chests) that hold Torah scrolls in synagogues throughout the world face Jerusalem.

- Jews end Passover Seders each year with the words: "Next year in Jerusalem"; the same words are pronounced at the end of Yom Kippur, the most solemn day of the Jewish year.

- A three-week moratorium on weddings in the summer recalls the breaching of the walls of Jerusalem by the Babylonian army in 586 BCE. That period culminates in a special day of mourning – Tisha B'Av (the 9th day of the Hebrew month Av) – commemorating the destruction of both the First and Second Temples.

- Jewish wedding ceremonies – a joyous occasion, is marked by sorrow over the loss of Jerusalem. The groom recites a biblical verse from the Babylonian Exile: "If I forget thee, O Jerusalem, let my right hand forget her cunning," and breaks a glass in commemoration of the destruction of the Temples.

Even 'body language', often said to tell volumes about a person, reflects the importance of Jerusalem to Jews as a people and, arguably, the lower priority the city holds for Muslims:

- When Jews pray they *face Jerusalem*; in Jerusalem they pray *facing the Temple Mount.*

- When Muslims pray, they *face Mecca*; in Jerusalem they pray with their *backs to the city.*

- Even at burial, a Muslim face, is turned toward Mecca.

Finally, consider the number of times 'Jerusalem' is mentioned in the two religions' holy books:

- The Old Testament mentions 'Jerusalem' 349 times. Zion, another name for 'Jerusalem,' is mentioned 108 times.[73]

- The Quran never mentions Jerusalem – *not even once.*

Even when others controlled Jerusalem, Jews maintained a physical presence in the city, despite being persecuted and impoverished. Before the advent of modern Zionism in the 1880s, Jews were moved by a form of religious Zionism to live in the Holy Land, settling particularly in four holy cities: Safed, Tiberias, Hebron, and most importantly – Jerusalem. Consequently, Jews constituted a majority of the city's population for generations. In 1898, "In this City of the Jews, where the Jewish population outnumbers all others three to one ..." Jews constituted 75 percent[74] of the Old City population in what Secretary-General Kofi Annan called 'East Jerusalem.' In 1914, when the Ottoman Turks

---

[73] See Ken Spiro, "Jerusalem: Jewish and Moslem Claims to the Holy City," at http://www.aish.com/Israel/articles/ _Jewish_and_Moslem_Claims_to_the_Holy_City.asp. (11341)

[74] "The eighty thousand Jews in Palestine, fully one-half are living within the walls, or in the twenty-three colonies just outside the walls, of Jerusalem. This number – forty thousand Jews in Jerusalem - is not an estimate carelessly made. ..." Edwin S. Wallace, Former U.S. Consul "The Jews in Jerusalem" *Cosmopolitan* magazine (1898; original pages of article are in possession of the author).

This document uses extensive links via the Internet. If you experience a broken link, please note the 5 digit number (xxxxx) at the end of the URL and use it as a Keyword in the Search Box at www.MEfacts.com.

44

ruled the city, 45,000 Jews made up a majority of the 65,000 residents. And at the time of Israeli statehood in 1948, 100,000 Jews lived in the city, compared to only 65,000 Arabs.[75] Prior to unification, Jordanian-controlled 'East Jerusalem' was a mere 6 square kilometers, compared to 38 square kilometers on the 'Jewish side.' Arab claims to Jerusalem, a Jewish city by all definitions, reflect the "what's-mine-is-mine, what's-yours-is-mine" mentality underlying Palestinian concepts and ICJ *encouragement* of how to end the Arab-Israeli conflict.

---

[75] "JERUSALEM - Whose City?" at http://christianactionforisrael.org/whosecity.html. (10744)

This document uses extensive links via the Internet. If you experience a broken link, please note the 5 digit number (xxxxx) at the end of the URL and use it as a Keyword in the Search Box at www.MEfacts.com.

4 Resolution 181 - the "Partition Plan"

The ICJ seeks to turn the UN General Assembly Resolution 181, that *recommended* the partition of the territory of Palestine (Partition Plan) into two states, one Jewish and one Arab, into a non-existent 'amendment' to the "Mandate for Palestine," thereby rewriting history and attempting to 'resurrect' Resolution 181.[76]

The Court's censored or careless 'legal review' of the status of the Territories, based on non-binding General Assembly resolutions, reaches its apex in the way the ICJ relates to a key UN document – the November 1947 General Assembly *recommendation*,[77] Resolution 181 – the "Partition Plan." While the Resolution was a non-binding recommendation, whose implementation hinged on acceptance by both parties, the ICJ views it as if it was a Security Council directive with the power to amend the above-mentioned international accords, irrespective of its acceptance by the parties.

---

[76] UN General Assembly Resolution 181 (II). Future government of Palestine. 29 November 1947. See at: http://www.mefacts.com/cache/html/un-resolutions/10063.htm. (10063)

[77] "*Appeals* to all Governments and all peoples to refrain from taking action which might hamper or delay the carrying out of these *recommendations* [to partition] ," UN Resolution 181, A, (d). [italics by author]

The ICJ cites Resolution 181 as one of the *legal pillars* supporting the right of Palestinian Arabs to self-determination alongside the "Mandate for Palestine."

It appears that the ICJ was unaware of the fact that in November 1947, all Arab States voted as a bloc against Resolution 181 and kept their *promise* to defy its implementation *by force*. Arab aggression is recorded in a host of UN documents, discussed elsewhere in this critique, regarding the *resuscitation* of Resolution 181 by the ICJ as a base for Palestinian rights to self-determination.

Aware of Arabs' past aggression, Resolution 181, in paragraph C, calls on the Security Council to:

> "… determine as a threat to the peace, breach of the peace or *act of aggression*, in accordance with Article 39 of the Charter, any attempt to *alter by force* the settlement envisaged by this resolution." [italics by author]

The ones who sought to alter by force the settlement envisioned in Resolution 181 were the Arabs who threatened *bloodshed* if the UN were to adopt the Resolution:

> "The Government of Palestine [E.H., that is, the British mandate government] fear that strife in Palestine will be greatly intensified when the Mandate is terminated, and that the international status of the United Nations Commission will mean little or nothing to the Arabs in Palestine, to whom *the killing of Jews now transcends all other considerations*. Thus, the Commission will be faced with the problem of how to avert certain *bloodshed* on a very much wider scale than prevails at present. … The Arabs have made it quite clear and have told the Palestine government that they do not propose to co-operate or to assist the Commission, and that, far from it, they *propose to attack and impede* its work in every possible way. We have no reason to suppose that they do not mean what they say."[78] [italics by author]

---

78 United Nations Palestine Commission, First Monthly Progress Report to the Security Council. A/AC.21/7, 29 January 1948. See: http://www.mefacts.com/cache/html/un-resolutions/10923.htm. (10923)

This document uses extensive links via the Internet. If you experience a broken link, please note the 5 digit number (xxxxx) at the end of the URL and use it as a Keyword in the Search Box at www.MEfacts.com.

Arabs' intentions and deeds did not fare better after Resolution 181 was adopted:

> "Taking into consideration that the Provisional Government of Israel has indicated its acceptance in principle of a prolongation of the truce in Palestine; that the States members of the Arab League have rejected successive appeals of the United Nations Mediator, and of the Security Council in its resolution 53 (1948) of 7 July 1948, for the prolongation of the truce in Palestine; and that there has consequently developed a renewal of hostilities in Palestine."[79]

Resolution 181 reads:

> "Having met in special session at the request of the mandatory Power to constitute and instruct a Special Committee to prepare for the consideration of the question of the future Government of Palestine. ... Having constituted a Special Committee and instructed it to investigate all questions and issues relevant to the problem of Palestine, and to prepare proposals for the solution of the problem, and Having received and examined the report of the Special Committee (document A/364). ... *Recommends* to the United Kingdom, as the mandatory Power for Palestine, and to all other Members of the United Nations the adoption and implementation, with regard to the future Government of Palestine, of the Plan of Partition with Economic Union set out below; ..." [italics by author].

The ICJ in its preamble states:

> "Recalling relevant General Assembly resolutions, including resolution 181 (II) of 29 November 1947, which partitioned mandated Palestine into two States, one Arab and one Jewish,"

In fact, Resolution 181 – was a *non-binding* resolution that only *recommended* partition. It *never* "partitioned" or "mandated" *anything* as the ICJ tries to inject.

The ICJ continues the discussion on the Partition Plan in paragraph 71 of the opinion:

> "In 1947 the United Kingdom announced its intention to complete

---

[79] See among others, Security Council Resolution S/RES/ 54 (1948) at http://www.mefacts.com/cache/html/un-resolutions/10894.htm. (10894)

This document uses extensive links via the Internet. If you experience a broken link, please note the 5 digit number (xxxxx) at the end of the URL and use it as a Keyword in the Search Box at www.MEfacts.com.

evacuation of the mandated territory by 1 August 1948, subsequently advancing that date to 15 May 1948. In the meantime, the General Assembly had on 29 November 1947 adopted resolution 181 (II) on the future government of Palestine, which 'Recommends to the United Kingdom ... and to all other Members of the United Nations the adoption and implementation ... of the Plan of Partition' of the territory, as set forth in the resolution, between two independent States, one Arab, the other Jewish, as well as the creation of a special international régime for the City of Jerusalem. The Arab population of Palestine and the Arab States rejected this plan, contending that it was unbalanced; on 14 May 1948, Israel proclaimed its independence on the strength of the General Assembly resolution; armed conflict then broke out between Israel and a number of Arab States and the Plan of Partition was not implemented."

The 1947 Partition Plan was the last of a *series of recommendations* that had been drawn up over the years by the Mandator and by international commissions, plans designed to reach an historic compromise between Arabs and Jews in western Palestine. The first was in 1922 when Great Britain unilaterally partitioned Palestine, but this did not satisfy the Arabs who wanted the entire country to be Arab. The 1947 Partition Plan followed such proposals as the Peel Commission (1937); the Woodhead Commission (1938); two 1946 proposals that championed a bi-national state; one proposed by the Anglo-American Committee of Inquiry in April 1946 based on a single state with equal powers for Jews and Arabs; and the Morrison-Grady Plan raised in July 1946 which recommended a federal state with two provinces – one Jewish, one Arab.

Every scheme since 1922 has been rejected by the Arab side, including decidedly pro-Arab recommendations. This was not because the suggestions were "unbalanced," as the ICJ *has been told* in Arab affidavits and stated in paragraph 71 of the Court opinion, but because these plans recognized the Jews as a nation and gave the Jewish citizens of Mandate Palestine political representation.

The ICJ's use of the term 'unbalanced' in describing the reason for Arab rejectionism of Resolution 181 hardly fits reality. 76 percent of the landmass of the original Mandate for the Jews was *excised* in 1922 to create a fourth Arab state – Transjordan (today Jordan).

David Lloyd George, then the British Prime Minister described the *recommendation* in resolution 181 rather differently than the ICJ describes. In his words:

> "… the Balfour Declaration implied that the whole of Palestine, including Transjordan, should ultimately become a Jewish state. Transjordan had, nevertheless, been severed from Palestine in 1922 and had subsequently been set up as an Arab kingdom. Now a second Arab state was to be carved out of the remainder of Palestine, with the result that the Jewish National Home would represent less than one eighth of the territory originally set aside for it. Such a sacrifice should not be asked of the Jewish people."[80]

Referring to the Arab States established as independent countries since the First World War, he said:

> "17,000,000 Arabs now occupied an area of 1,290,000 square miles, including all the principal Arab and Moslem centres, while Palestine, after the loss of Transjordan, was only 10,000 square miles; yet the majority plan proposed to reduce it by one half. UNSCOP proposed to eliminate Western Galilee from the Jewish State; that was *an injustice and a grievous* handicap to the development of the *Jewish State.*"[81] [italics by author]

The ICJ assumes that Resolution 181 legally amended and superseded the terms of the Mandate and that Israel's independence is a result of a partial implementation of the Partition Plan.

The ICJ Bench states in paragraph 71 of its opinion that:

> "… on 14 May 1948, Israel proclaimed its independence on the strength of the General Assembly resolution."

While factually ("on the strength") this is true, the resolution has *no legal ramifications* – that is, Resolution 181 recognized the Jewish right to statehood, but its validity as a potentially legal and binding document was never consummated. Like the schemes that preceded it, Resolution

---

[80] Yearbook of the United Nations 1947-48. 1949.I.13. 31 December 1948. See at: http://www.mefacts.com/cache/html/un-documents/11270.htm. (11270)

[81] Ibid.

This document uses extensive links via the Internet. If you experience a broken link, please note the 5 digit number (xxxxx) at the end of the URL and use it as a Keyword in the Search Box at www.MEfacts.com.

181's validity hinged on acceptance by *both parties* of the General Assembly's recommendation.

Cambridge Professor Sir Elihu Lauterpacht, Judge ad hoc of the International Court of Justice, a renowned expert on international law and editor of one of the 'bibles' of international law, *Oppenheim's International Law*, clarified that from a legal standpoint: The 1947 UN Partition Resolution had no legislative character to vest territorial rights in either Jews or Arabs. In a monograph relating to one of the most complex aspects of the territorial issue, the status of Jerusalem,[82] Judge, Sir Lauterpacht wrote that any binding force the Partition Plan would have, had to arise from the principle *pacta sunt servanda*,[83] that is, from agreement of the parties at variance to the proposed plan. In the case of Israel, Judge, Sir Lauterpacht explains:

> "... the coming into existence of Israel does not depend legally upon the Resolution. The right of a State to exist flows from its factual existence – especially when that existence is prolonged, shows every sign of continuance and is recognised by the generality of nations."

Reviewing Lauterpacht's arguments, Professor Stone, a distinguished authority on the Law of Nations, added that Israel's "legitimacy" or the "legal foundation" for its birth does not reside with the United Nations' Partition Plan, which as a consequence of Arab actions became a dead issue. Professor Stone concluded:

> "... The State of Israel is thus not legally derived from the partition plan, but rests (as do most other states in the world) on assertion of independence by its people and government, on the vindication of that independence by arms against assault by other states, and on the establishment of orderly government within territory under its stable control."[84]

---

[82] Professor, Judge Sir Elihu Lauterpacht, "Jerusalem and the Holy Places," Pamphlet No. 19 (London, Anglo-Israel Association, 1968).

[83] "Treaties must be honored," the first principle of international law.

[84] Professor Julius Stone, "Israel and Palestine, Assault on the Law of Nations" *The Johns Hopkins University Press*, 1981, p. 127.

Such attempts by Palestinians (and now by the ICJ) to 'roll back the clock' and resuscitate Resolution 181 more than five decades after they rejected it 'as if nothing had happened,' are totally inadmissible. Both Palestinians and their Arab brethren in neighboring countries rendered the plan null and void by their own subsequent aggressive actions.

Arabs absolute rejectionism of Resolution 181.

Following passage of Resolution 181 by the General Assembly, Arab countries took the dais to reiterate their absolute rejection of the recommendation and intention to render implementation of Resolution 181 a moot question by the use of force. These examples from the transcript of the General Assembly plenary meeting on 29, November 1947 speak for themselves:

> "Mr. JAMALI (Iraq): ... We believe that the decision which we have now taken ... undermines peace, justice and democracy. In the name of my Government, I wish to state that it feels that this decision is antidemocratic, illegal, impractical and contrary to the Charter ... Therefore, in the name of my Government, I wish to put on record that Iraq does not recognize the validity of this decision, will reserve freedom of action towards its implementation, and holds those who were influential in passing it against the free conscience of mankind responsible for the consequences."

> "Amir. ARSLAN (Syria): ... Gentlemen, the Charter is dead. But it did not die a natural death; it was murdered, and you all know who is guilty. My country will never recognize such a decision [Partition]. It will never agree to be responsible for it. Let the consequences be on the heads of others, not on ours."

> "H. R. H. Prince Seif El ISLAM ABDULLAH (Yemen): The Yemen delegation has stated previously that the partition plan is contrary to justice and to the Charter of the United Nations. Therefore, the Government of Yemen does not consider itself bound by such a decision ... and will reserve its freedom of action towards the implementation of this decision."[85]

---

[85] UN GA "Continuation of the discussion on the Palestinian question." Hundred and twenty-eighth plenary meeting. A/PV.128, 29 November, 1947. (11363)

This document uses extensive links via the Internet. If you experience a broken link, please note the 5 digit number (xxxxx) at the end of the URL and use it as a Keyword in the Search Box at www.MEfacts.com.

The Partition Plan was met not only by *verbal* rejection on the Arab side but also by concrete, bellicose steps to block its implementation and destroy the Jewish polity by force of arms, a goal the Arabs publicly declared even before Resolution 181 was brought to a vote.

Moreover, the ICJ simply ignores the *unpleasant fact* that the Arabs not only rejected the compromise and took action to prevent establishment of a Jewish state but also blocked establishment of an Arab state under the partition plan not just *before* the Israel War of Independence, but also *after* the war when they themselves controlled the West Bank (1948-1967), rendering the *recommendation* a still birth.

Professor Stone wrote about this novelty of resurrection in 1981 when he analyzed a similar attempt by pro-Palestinians 'experts' at the UN to rewrite the history of the conflict (published as 'Studies'). Stone called it "revival of the dead":

> "To attempt to show, as these studies do, that Resolution 181(II) 'remains' in force in 1981 is thus an undertaking even more *miraculous* than would be the *revival of the dead.* It is an attempt to give life to an entity that the Arab states had themselves aborted before it came to maturity and birth. To propose that Resolution 181(II) can be treated as if it has binding force in 1981, [E.H. the year Professor Stone's book was published] for the benefit of the same Arab states, who by their aggression destroyed it *ab initio,*[86] also violates 'general principles of law,' such as those requiring claimants to equity to come 'with clean hands,' and forbidding a party who has unlawfully repudiated a transaction from holding the other party to terms that suit the later expediencies of the repudiating party."[87]

In its narrative of events, the International Court of Justice's opinion does not even mention the fact that Jordan (at the time, Transjordan) crossed the international border (the Jordan River) and illegally occupied part of Mandate Palestine, annexing and labeling it the 'West Bank' to make it sound like a natural part of the 'east bank'

---

[86] In Latin: From the beginning.
[87] Professor Julius Stone, "Israel and Palestine, Assault on the Law of Nations" The Johns Hopkins University Press, 1981, p. 128.

(Transjordan). Indeed, it was Jordan that controlled the West Bank for 19 years between 1948 and 1967.[88]

How does the ICJ describe these scores of events?

"The Plan of Partition was not implemented."[89]

The ICJ fails to read the *fine print* in the Resolutions it cites. The ICJ embraces the General Assembly's generous annexation of Jerusalem (discussed later in this critique) as part of 'Occupied Palestinian Territory' – constantly referring to "the Occupied Palestinian Territories, including East Jerusalem." In the same breath, the ICJ cites Resolution 181 that leaves the status of Jerusalem in abeyance, in Part III (D) calling for a temporary 'special regime' for the City of Jerusalem:

> "… not later than 1 October 1948. It shall remain in force in the first instance for a period of ten years, unless the Trusteeship Council finds it necessary to undertake a re-examination of these provisions at an earlier date. After the expiration of this period the whole scheme shall be subject to re-examination by the Trusteeship Council in the light of the experience acquired with its functioning. The residents of the City shall be then free to express by means of a referendum their wishes as to possible modifications of the regime of the City."

Again, this never took place because the Partition Plan became a dead issue. If it is not a dead issue, logically, after 56 years it is time to call for

---

[88] "The 1948 Arab-Israeli War – Prior to the UN General Assembly's November 1947 decision to partition Palestine, King Abdullah had proposed sending the Arab Legion to defend the Arabs of Palestine. Reacting to the passing of the partition plan, he announced Jordan's readiness to deploy the full force of the Arab Legion in Palestine. An Arab League meeting held in Amman two days before the expiration of the British mandate concluded that Arab countries would send troops to Palestine to join forces with Jordan's army. … [Jordan] Parliament unanimously approved a motion to unite the two banks of the Jordan River, constitutionally expanding the Hashemite Kingdom of Jordan in order to safeguard what was left of the Arab territory of Palestine from further Zionist expansion." See the official Hashemite Kingdom of Jordan website at: http://www.kinghussein.gov.jo/his_palestine.html. (10634)

[89] See paragraph 71 of the ICJ's ruling at: http://middleeastfacts.org/content/ICJ/ICJ-Ruling-HTML.htm. (10908)

a referendum (as stated in Resolution 181, see above) of all Jerusalemites, Jews and Arabs, to decide the status of the city that has always had a Jewish majority as far back as 1870.

Even the UN recognized that Resolution 181 was a moot issue. Had the ICJ examined UN records, it would have had to address a July 30, 1949 working paper of the UN Secretariat, entitled *The Future of Arab Palestine and the Question of Partition,* which noted that:

> "The Arabs rejected the United Nations Partition Plan so that any comment of theirs did not specifically concern the status of the Arab section of Palestine under partition but rather rejected the scheme in its entirety.

> "... On 18 September the Progress Report of the Mediator was submitted to the General Assembly. In evaluating the situation of the proposed Arab State, the Mediator stated: 'As regards the parts of Palestine under Arab control, no central authority exists and no independent Arab State has been organized or attempted. This situation may be explained in part by Arab unwillingness to undertake any step which would suggest even tacit acceptance of partition, and by their insistence on a unitary State in Palestine. The Partition Plan presumed that effective organs of state government could be more or less immediately set up in the Arab part of Palestine. This does not seem possible today in view of the lack of organized authority springing from Arab Palestine itself, and the administrative disintegration following the termination of the Mandate.'"[90]

The Secretariat considered Resolution 181 a dead issue, noting:

> "... an Arab State for which the Partition Plan provided has not materialized ..."[91]

In the eyes of the International Court of Justice, even the 1948 Israel War of Independence – *before the occupation* and clearly an Arab war of aggression – gets the same treatment as the Six-Day War of 1967. The ICJ's rendition of events exonerates the Arabs of any complicity, skipping merrily over uncomfortable facts in the process:

---

[90] United Nations Conciliation Commission for Palestine: The Future of Arab Palestine and the Question of Partition. A/AC.25/W.19, 30 July 1949. See: http://www.mefacts.com/cache/html/un-documents/11070.htm. (11070)

[91] Ibid.

This document uses extensive links via the Internet. If you experience a broken link, please note the 5 digit number (xxxxx) at the end of the URL and use it as a Keyword in the Search Box at www.MEfacts.com.

"The Arab population of Palestine and the Arab States rejected the [Partition] plan, contending that it was *unbalanced*; on 14 May 1948, Israel proclaimed its independence on the strength of the General Assembly resolution; armed conflict then broke out between Israel and a number of Arab States and the Plan of Partition was not implemented."[92] [italics by author]

Far more significantly, from 1922 forward and through nearly three decades of British Mandatory rule, the Arabs systematically rejected every plan for co-existence that included any form of Jewish political empowerment whatsoever. These plans included British attempts to create a joint legislature, insuring the Arabs would have had an overwhelming majority and that they could have cut off any further Jewish immigration. These same Arabs even refused to establish an Arab Agency for development of the Arab sector, which would parallel the Jewish Agency.[93]

In the fall of 1947, the UN Ad Hoc Committee on Palestinian Question[94] tried, to no avail, to 'bring the Arabs around.' Had the ICJ read the minutes of this damning UN document, they would find this rejectionism clearly established. The Special Rapporteur, Thor Thors of Iceland, wrote to the Security Council days before the historic vote on November 25, 1947. He cited how the Arab Higher Committee first:

"… rejected the recommendations of the Special Committee on Palestine and advocated the establishment on democratic lines, in the whole of Palestine, of an Arab State which would protect the legitimate rights and interests of all minorities."[95]

and later:

"… did not accept an invitation to … discussed the question of boundaries.

---

[92] Paragraph 71 of the Court's ruling. See: http://middleeastfacts.org/content/ICJ/ICJ-Ruling-HTML.htm. (10908)

[93] Christopher Sykes, Cross Roads to Israel – Palestine from Balfour to Bevin, Collins London 1965, p. 81.

[94] General Assembly, A/516, 25 November 1947, at http://www.mefacts.com/cache/html/un-documents/11290.htm. (11290)

[95] Ibid.

This document uses extensive links via the Internet. If you experience a broken link, please note the 5 digit number (xxxxx) at the end of the URL and use it as a Keyword in the Search Box at www.MEfacts.com.

> The Arab Higher Committee was prepared to assist and furnish information only with regard to the question of the termination of the Mandate and the creation of a unitary State."[96]

As mentioned before, the Arabs threatened *bloodshed* if the UN adopted Resolution 181 (The Partition Plan, recommending the creation of an Jewish state and an Arab state) and then voted as a bloc against Resolution 181, keeping their 'promise' to defy its implementation by force.

Suffice it to say, the use of the terms "rejection" and "contending" in the ICJ's 'historical narrative' hardly befit 1948 realities. "Rejection" was expressed in nearly six months of guerrilla warfare by local Arabs (today's Palestinians) against the Jews of Palestine (today's Israelis), targeting primarily civilians. In the midst of this period (January 29, 1948), the First Monthly Progress Report of the UN-appointed Palestine Commission was submitted to the Security Council. How does the UN describe what actually transpired?

Actualization of Resolution 181 was placed in the hands of a

> "commission … with direct responsibility for implementing the measures recommended by the General Assembly."[97]

Implementation of Resolution 181 hinged not only on the five Member States appointed to represent the UN (Bolivia, Czechoslovakia, Denmark, Panama, Philippines) and Great Britain, but first and foremost on the participation of the *two sides* who were invited to appoint representatives. The Commission than reported:

> "… The invitation extended by the [181] resolution was promptly accepted by the Government of the United Kingdom and by the Jewish Agency for Palestine, both of which designated representatives to assist the commission.

---

[96] In lieu of the two independent States, the city of Jerusalem under an international regime, and the economic union proposed.

[97] United Nations Palestine Commission. First Monthly Progress Report To The Security Council. A/AC.21/7. 29 January 1948. See at: http://www.mefacts.com/cache/html/un-resolutions/10923.htm. (10923)

This document uses extensive links via the Internet. If you experience a broken link, please note the 5 digit number (xxxxx) at the end of the URL and use it as a Keyword in the Search Box at www.MEfacts.com.

... As regards [to] the Arab Higher Committee, the following telegraphic response was received by the Secretary-General on 19 January:

ARAB HIGHER COMMITTEE IS DETERMINED PRESIST [PERSIST] IN REJECTION PARTITION AND IN REFUSAL RECOGNIZE UN[O] RESOLUTION THIS RESPECT AND ANYTHING DERIVING THEREFROM [THERE FROM]. FOR THESE REASONS IT IS UNABLE [TO] ACCEPT [THE] INVITATION."[98]

The fact that Resolution 181 was a non-binding *recommendation* is clearly reflected in the language of the report, which declares, "... the full implementation of the Assembly's *recommendations* requires the presence of the commission in Palestine" and speaks of an "invitation" to all the parties concerned to accept the scheme and bring it to fruition.

ICJ - "Armed conflict then broke out"

The "armed conflict [that] then broke out,"[99] in the words of the International Court of Justice, was Israel's War of Independence, actually the *second* stage of this Arab war of aggression, launched the day after Israel's acceptance of Resolution 181 on November 29, 1947. It was a pre-planned and coordinated invasion by the armed forces of Egypt, Transjordan, Syria, Lebanon, Iraq, and contingents from Saudi Arabia and Yemen forces across the international borders of Mandate Palestine, boasting they would "throw the Jews into the sea." Numerous UN documents leave no doubt of this.

On May 22, 1948, in response to an urgent cablegram to the Lebanese foreign minister from the Security Council inquiring whether Lebanon had invaded, the foreign minister wrote the Security Council:

"[Lebanese forces] are operating in northern Palestine. Their military objectives are to help pacify Palestine in cooperation with the forces of other States of the Arab League, as stated in the memorandum of the

---

[98] Ibid.

[99] Paragraph 71 of the Court's ruling. See: http://middleeastfacts.org/content/ICJ/ICJ-Ruling-HTML.htm. (10908)

This document uses extensive links via the Internet. If you experience a broken link, please note the 5 digit number (xxxxx) at the end of the URL and use it as a Keyword in the Search Box at www.MEfacts.com.

Secretary-General of the Arab League on May 1 (document S/745). ... The League of Arab States is responsible for the exercise of political functions in any and all parts of Palestine. ... The League of Arab States is not now negotiating with the Jews on a political settlement in Palestine and will not enter into such negotiations so long as the Jews persist in their intention and their efforts to establish a Jewish state in Palestine."[100]

On May 18, 1948 in response to a similar cablegram to the Iraqi delegate to the UN, the reply was that indeed there were Iraqi troops in Palestine in areas where Jews are the majority, declaring that

"... Elements of our armed forces entered Palestine without discrimination either to the character of areas or to the creed of the inhabitants [invaded Jewish areas] ... Units of Iraqi forces are now operating west of the Jordan. ... Their military objectives ... are the suppression of lawless Zionist terrorism which was dangerously spreading all over the country, and restoration of peace and order. Such objectives will result in enabling the people of Palestine to set up a 'united state' in which both Arabs and Jews will enjoy equal Democratic rights. ... Upon the termination of the Mandate on the 15th May, 1948, no legal authority was constituted to take its place. In the same time the terrorism and the aggression of a minority assumed vast proportions and resulted in atrocities and massacre leading up to a complete state of anarchy. ... The Arab League, as a regional organization interested in keeping the peace in that region could not stand by without action. ... Concerning what is called areas (Towns, cities, districts) of Palestine where Jews are in the majority, it must again be stated that the division of the country into such units for the present purpose is misleading and can be entertained on the basis of partition which we reject."[101]

A similar query to the foreign minister of Transjordan was ignored. The following questions were not answered:

"Are armed element of your armed forces or irregular forces sponsored by

---

[100] United Nations Security Council Document S/770, 22 May 1948, at: http://domino. un.org/unispal.nsf/9a798adbf322aff38525617b006d88d7/98be7a17e488f06985256db20 0676705!OpenDocument. (11364)

[101] United Nations Security Council Document S/769 22 May, 1948. See: http:// domino.un.org/unispal.nsf/9a798adbf322aff38525617b006d88d7/65eb4dccbb362b5585 256e4c006f6a02!OpenDocument (11365)

This document uses extensive links via the Internet. If you experience a broken link, please note the 5 digit number (xxxxx) at the end of the URL and use it as a Keyword in the Search Box at www.MEfacts.com.

your government now operating (1) in Palestine (2) in areas (towns, cities, districts) of Palestine where the Jews are in the majority?"[102]

Instead the Transjordanian foreign minister complained in a short cablegram that

"the government of the United States of America [who had penned the questions for the Security Council] has not yet recognized the government of the Hashemite Kingdom of Transjordan ... yet [it] recognized the so-called Jewish government within a few hours ..."

The Arabs rejected repeated calls by the Security Council for a cease-fire and only agreed to a four-week truce after being warned by the Security Council on May 29, 1948:

"... if the present resolution is rejected by either party or by both, or if, having been accepted, it is subsequently repudiated or violated, the situation in Palestine will be reconsidered with a view to action under Chapter VII of the Charter."[103]

The first cease-fire in the 18-month war finally took effect on June 11, 1948. The documents cited above are only a few examples of the evidence available to the ICJ, all of which appear to have been ignored.

Israel overcomes Arab aggression at a terrible cost.

While Israel prevailed, one percent of the pre-war Jewish population (6,000 persons) was killed. In American terms, that is equivalent to 2.8 million American civilians and soldiers being killed over an 18-month period.[104] The facts that there were a clear aggressor and a clear target in the

---

[102] Security Council Document S/760, 20 May 2003 (the date is incorrect in the original), http://domino.un.org/unispal.nsf/9a798adbf322aff38525617b006d88d7/aa99ba96c0a95 d5985256db2006928bd!OpenDocument. (11366)

[103] Security Council Document S/801, 29 May 1948, at: http://domino.un.org/ unispal.nsf/9a798adbf322aff38525617b006d88d7/34235b8f785c7b4485256e76006e58 da!OpenDocument. (11367)

[104] Between November 30, 1947 – July 20, 1949.

This document uses extensive links via the Internet. If you experience a broken link, please note the 5 digit number (xxxxx) at the end of the URL and use it as a Keyword in the Search Box at www.MEfacts.com.

"armed conflict" in 1948 appears in a host of UN documents that are as immaterial in the International Court of Justice's eyes as the fate of over a thousand Israelis, again, mostly civilians, murdered in cold blood by Palestinian suicide bombers and other terrorists since 2000. These latest killings precipitated the building of a non lethal security barrier.

What became of Resolution 181? On May 17, 1948 – after the invasion began – the Palestine Commission designed to implement Resolution 181 adjourned *sine die* [indefinitely], after the General Assembly:

> "appointed a United Nations Mediator in Palestine, which relieves the United Nations Palestine Commission from the further exercise of its responsibilities."

At the time, some thought the partition plan could be revived, but by the end of the war, Resolution 181 had become a moot issue as realities on the ground made establishment of an armistice-line (the Green Line), a temporary ceasefire line expected to be followed by peace treaties, the most constructive path to solving the conflict.

The Palestinians, for their part, continued to reject Resolution 181, viewing the Jewish state as "occupied territory," a label that exists to this day in PLO and Palestinian Authority maps, insignias and even statistical data. Rejection of any form of Jewish polity anywhere in western Palestine was underscored in the PLO's 1964 Charter.

The Arab Palestinians and the 'Clean Hand' principle.

Only a few years ago voices were suddenly heard in Arab circles that the Partition Plan should be the basis of a "just and lasting peace," rather than demanding a return to the Green Line. The ICJ is the first highly regarded institution to *fall for the bait,* claiming that Palestinian rights to self-determination emanate from the very document repudiated by the Arabs for more than fifty years. In 1976, for example, the Arab League was still berating the 'Family of Nations' at the UN that: "In its resolution 181(II) of 29 November 1947, the General Assembly imposed the partition on Palestine against the expressed wishes of the majority of its population."[105]

The International Court of Justice, which accepted testimony from the Palestinians as interested parties and declared that it is the ICJ's solemn responsibility to stand up for Palestinian rights, performs another flip-flop, declaring that in such instances (i.e. the "clean hands" test) the Palestinians are exempt, having no standing in the case. In paragraphs 63 and 64 of the opinion, the ICJ says:

> "Israel has contended that Palestine, given its responsibility for acts of violence against Israel and its population which the wall is aimed at addressing, cannot seek from the Court a remedy for a situation resulting from its own wrongdoing. In this context, Israel has invoked the *maxim nullus commodum capere potest de sua injuria propria*, which it considers to be as relevant in advisory proceedings as it is in contentious cases. Therefore, Israel concludes, good faith and the principle of 'clean hands' provide a compelling reason that should lead the Court to refuse the General Assembly's request. The Court does not consider this argument [the 'clean hands' argument raised by Israel] to be pertinent. As was emphasized earlier, it was the General Assembly which requested the advisory opinion, and the opinion is to be given to the General Assembly, and not to a specific State or entity."

Professor Stone explains the 'clean hands' concept:

> "… there are also certain other legal grounds, rooted in basic notions of justice and equity, on which the Arab states (and the Palestinians whom they represented in these matters) should not, in any case, be permitted, after so lawless a resort to violence against the plan, to turn around decades later, and claim legal entitlements under it.

> "More than one of 'the general principles of law' acknowledged in Article 38(1)(c) of the Statute of the International Court of Justice seem to forbid it. Such claimants do not come with 'clean hands' to seek equity; their hands indeed are mired by their lawlessly violent bid to destroy the very resolution

---

[105] At a meeting of the Committee on the Exercise of the Inalienable Rights of the Palestinians People, General Assembly Document A/AC.183/L.22, April 26, 1976, at: http://domino.un.org/UNISPAL.NSF/0/842f480902f25fef85256e2f006a82d2?OpenDocument. (11374)

This document uses extensive links via the Internet. If you experience a broken link, please note the 5 digit number (xxxxx) at the end of the URL and use it as a Keyword in the Search Box at www.MEfacts.com.

[181] and plan from which they now seek equity. They may also be thought by their representations concerning these documents, to have led others to act to their own detriment, and thus to be debarred by their own conduct from espousing, in pursuit of present expediencies, positions they formerly so strongly denounced. They may also be thought to be in breach of the general principle of good faith in two other respects.

"Their position resembles that of a party to a transaction who has unlawfully repudiated the transaction, and comes to court years later claiming that selected provisions of it should be meticulously enforced against the wronged party. It also resembles that of a party who has by unlawful violence wilfully destroyed the subject-matter that is 'the fundamental basis' on which consent rested, and now clamors to have the original terms enforced against the other party. These are grounds that reinforce the pithy view of U.S. Legal Adviser Herbert Hansell that the 1947 partition was never effectuated.

"… the Partition Resolution and Plan, since they were prevented by Arab rejection and armed aggression from entering into legal operation, could not thereafter carry any legal effects binding on Israel."[106]

The International Court of Justice insists that as a UN institution it must take the case of the security fence, based on two major documents – one that is *totally misunderstood* by the ICJ – the "Mandate for Palestine" – and the other that it seeks to *resurrect* – UN General Assembly Resolution 181 [The Partition Plan].

When armistice lines were finally drawn, in the spring and summer of 1949, under the auspices of the UN, they reflected 'facts on the ground.'

In closing, Resolution 181 had been tossed into the waste bin of history, along with the Partition Plans.

---

[106] Professor Julius Stone, "Israel and Palestine, Assault on the Law of Nations" p.65, The Johns Hopkins University Press, 1981.

5 UN Charter, Article 51 - 'Customized'

The ICJ Bench ignored repeated acts of terrorism from Palestine as emanating from non-State entities and therefore inadmissible to the issue of the security fence. The Court 'assigned' Israel total control as an "Occupying Power" by ignoring the existence of the Palestinian Authority.

The ICJ's opinion engages in some highly questionable interpretations not only of its own mandate, but also the UN Charter's article on the right to self-defence, or in the case of Israel – the lack of the right to self-defence. The worst of all statements concerns a *fallacious interpretation* of Article 51 of the UN Charter.

The ICJ writes in paragraph 139 of the opinion:

"Under the terms of Article 51 of the Charter of the United Nations:

'Nothing in the present Charter shall impair the inherent right of individual or collective self-defence if an armed attack occurs against a Member of the United Nations, until the Security Council has taken measures necessary to maintain international peace and security.'

"Article 51 of the Charter thus recognizes the existence of an inherent right of self-defence in the case of armed attack by *one State against another State*. However, Israel does not claim that the attacks against it are imputable to a foreign State. ... Consequently, the Court concludes that *Article 51 of the Charter has no relevance in this case.*" [italics by author]

Article 51 of the UN Charter clearly recognizes "the inherent right of individual or collective self-defence" *by anyone.* That is, the language of Article 51 does not identify or stipulate the kind of aggressor or aggressors against whom this right of self-defence can be exercised ... and certainly does not limit the right to self-defence to attacks by States!

ICJ also ignores the fact that Palestinian warfare is "... strictly regulated by the customs and provisions of the law of armed conflict, referred to here as international humanitarian law (IHL)."

> "The authoritative commentary of the ICRC to the Fourth Geneva Convention justifies applying the provision to *non-state actors,* saying [t]here can be no drawbacks in this, since the Article in its reduced form, contrary to what might be thought, *does not in any way limit the right* [E.H. to self-defence] *of a State to put down rebellion,* nor does it increase in the slightest the authority of the rebel [Palestinian Authority] party ..."[107] [italics by author]

The ICJ ignores the Palestinian Authority (PA) violations of their assumed responsibility, such as the Oslo Accords, that required the Palestinians to abide by internationally recognized human rights standards. The Israeli Palestinian interim agreement of September 28, 1995 stated:

> "Israel and the Council [Palestinian Interim Self-Government Authority, i.e. the elected Council,] hereinafter 'the Council' or 'the Palestinian Council' shall exercise their powers and responsibilities pursuant to this Agreement with due regard to internationally-accepted norms and principles of human rights and the rule of law."[108]

---

[107] See Legal Standards in "Erased In A Moment: Suicide Bombing Attacks Against Israeli Civilians," HRW, October 2002 at: http://www.hrw.org/reports/2002/isrl-pa/index. htm#TopOfPage. (11262)

See also ICRC "...the right of a State to put down rebellion." In "Article 3 - Conflicts not of an International Character" at: http://www.icrc.org/ihl.nsf/0/1919123e0d121fefc12563 cd0041fc08?OpenDocument. (11368)

[108] Under "Israeli-Palestinian Interim Agreement on the West Bank and the Gaza Strip," Article XIX, Human Rights and the Rule of Law. September 28, 1995. See: http://www.mfa.gov.il/MFA/Peace%20Process/Guide%20to%20the%20Peace%20Proces s/THE%20ISRAELI-PALESTINIAN%20INTERIM%20AGREEMENT#art13. (10944)

This document uses extensive links via the Internet. If you experience a broken link, please note the 5 digit number (xxxxx) at the end of the URL and use it as a Keyword in the Search Box at www.MEfacts.com.

Both under the "international humanitarian law" and the 'Oslo Accord' Israel rights to self defence under Article 51 can not be more apparent.

Nothing can be more ludicrous than the ICJ conclusion that because "Israel does not claim that the attacks [by Palestinian terrorists] against it are imputable to a foreign State" Israel *lost* its right to act in self-defence.

It is worth to note that the UN and its organs have compromised even the Geneva Convention's protocols, by selective politicization to bash Israel.[109] The High Contracting Parties never met once to discuss Cambodia's killing fields or the 800,000 Rwandans murdered in the course of three months in 1994.[110] *Israel is the only country in the Geneva Convention's 52-year history to be the object of a country-specific denunciation.*

The ICJ lacks the authority to amend or 'interpret' Article 51.

There is no foundation for 'adding restrictions,' narrowly interpreting Article 51's meaning, or simply making changes to the UN Charter. The ICJ neglects to reference Articles 108 and 109 of the UN Charter that set the precedent rules for amending the Charter:

> "Amendments to the present Charter shall come into force for all Members [E.H. and not a customized version for Israel] of the United Nations when they have been adopted by a vote of two thirds of the members of the General Assembly and ratified in accordance with their respective constitutional processes by two thirds of the Members of the United Nations, including all the permanent members of the Security Council."

---

[109] For the text of the February 9, 1999 resolution "Illegal Israeli actions in Occupied East Jerusalem and the rest of the Occupied Palestinian Territory," see: http://www.mefacts.com/cache/html/un-resolutions/11124.htm. (11124)

[110] See Associated Press report "More Than One Million Rwandans Killed in 1990's," *New York Times*, February 16, 2002 at http://www.mtholyoke.edu/acad/intrel/bush/rwandadeaths.htm. (10731)

This document uses extensive links via the Internet. If you experience a broken link, please note the 5 digit number (xxxxx) at the end of the URL and use it as a Keyword in the Search Box at www.MEfacts.com.

It is rather strange that the ICJ, of all bodies, takes liberties to change what Article 51 clearly states. This ICJ also failed to review its own past writings on the subject of *attempting to interpret* UN Charter Articles. Elsewhere in the opinion, the ICJ quotes its 1950 ruling on South West Africa (Namibia) regarding Article 80 of the same UN Charter, saying that Articles of the UN Charter were carefully penned and should be strictly read in a direct manner 'as is':

> "The Court considered that if Article … had been intended to create an obligation … such intention would have been *expressed in a direct manner*."[111] [italics by author)

The ICJ Bench zig-zags from strict construction to loose construction, coupled with biased *interpretation* to deny Israel the fundamental right to defend its citizens from terrorism.

Writing on the subject of the *legal effect of Resolutions and Codes of Conduct of the United Nations* Judge Schwebel, a past President of the ICJ, notes:

> "what the terms and the *travaux* (notes for the official record) of the Charter do not support can scarcely be implemented."[112]

Ironically, in December 2004, the UN High-level Panel on Threats, Challenges and Change, published the much anticipated report entitled "A more secure world our shared resonsibility." Paragraph 192 of this report states:

> **"We do not favour the rewriting or reinterpretation of Article 51."** [Bold in the original]

The same is true of the International Court of Justice, which lack the mandate to 'amend' Article 51.

---

[111] See International status of South-West Africa. Advisory Opinion of 11 July 1950 at: http://www.icj-cij.org/icjwww/idecisions/isummaries/isswasummary500711.htm. (10954)

[112] Professor, Judge Stephen M. Schwebel, *The Legal Effect of Resolutions and Codes of Conduct of the United Nations* in "Justice in International Law", Cambridge University Press, 1994. Opinions quoted in this critiques are not derived from his position as a judge of the ICJ.

This document uses extensive links via the Internet. If you experience a broken link, please note the 5 digit number (xxxxx) at the end of the URL and use it as a Keyword in the Search Box at www.MEfacts.com.

6 Terrorism

UN-sponsored International Conventions, Security Council Resolutions, and the Report of the Secretary-General prepared pursuant to General Assembly Resolution ES-10/13 on Terrorism, are all *immaterial* to the ICJ.

The ICJ fails to examine even one of the United Nation's own conventions and covenants that define terrorism, the root cause of the construction of the security fence, and what one may and may not do to combat it.

What makes this all the more ironic is the fact that the ICJ cites UN Document A/ES-10/248 - the report of the Secretary General on the security fence as a key document and source of information for its opinion. Yet the ICJ ignores entirely the points in the Secretary-General's Report[113] that admits the causal relationship between *terrorism*

---

[113] UN Document A/ES-10/248, November 24, 2003, "Report of the Secretary-General prepared pursuant to General Assembly resolution ES-10/13," November 24, 2003, at: http://domino.un.org/unispal.nsf/0/a5a017029c05606b85256dec00626057?Open Document. (10575)

This document uses extensive links via the Internet. If you experience a broken link, please note the 5 digit number (xxxxx) at the end of the URL and use it as a Keyword in the Search Box at www.MEfacts.com.

and the security barrier in Section C (Route of the Barrier) (4) of his report – a fact that can hardly be reconciled with the ICJ's conclusion that the barrier is wholly political.

The Secretary-General report's cites:

> "... After a sharp rise in Palestinian terror attacks in the spring of 2002, the [Israeli] Cabinet approved Government Decision 64/B on 14 April 2002, which called for construction of 80 kilometers of the Barrier in the three areas of the West Bank."

Not only does the report label the Palestinian actions as *terror*, but it also clearly establishes, in its own words, the cause for building a security barrier. The ICJ completely ignores this fact; at no point is it mentioned in the ICJ's opinion.[114]

In December 1997, the United Nations adopted Resolution 52/164[115] – *the International Convention for the Suppression of Terrorist Bombings* – a contribution to international law that establishes rules of jurisdiction in the prosecution of terrorists. The UN legislation clearly defines terrorism and 'who is a terrorist,' declaring, for the first time, that:

> "... the States Members of the United Nations solemnly reaffirm their unequivocal condemnation of all acts, methods and practices of terrorism as criminal and unjustifiable, *wherever* and by *whomever* committed." [italics by author]

This text is clear as a bell: Regarding *any* act of terrorism, the ends do not justify the means.

Article 2 of Resolution 52/164 defines a terrorist as:

> "*Any* person [who] unlawfully and intentionally delivers, places, discharges or detonates an explosive or other lethal device in, into or against a place of

---

114 Report of the Secretary-General prepared pursuant to General Assembly resolution ES-10/13, 21 October 2003, paragraph C, 1. (11317)

115 UN General Assembly, International Convention for the Suppression of Terrorist Bombings, Adopted without a vote, 15 December 1997. See: http://www.un.org/ga/documents/gares52/res52164.htm. (10899)

public use, a State or government facility, a public transportation system or an infrastructure facility … with the intent to cause death or serious bodily injury … or with the intent to cause extensive destruction of such a place, facility or system, where such destruction results in or is likely to result in major economic loss."[116]

It underscores in 2 a-c, that this includes:

"… accomplices, organizers and directors and other persons who in any other way contribute to the commission of such acts."

There is no *escape clause* in this piece of international law that exempts "struggles for self-determination" from anti-terrorism resolutions. In fact, the International Convention for the Suppression of Terrorist Bombings clarifies in Article 11 that:

"None of the offences set forth in article 2 shall be regarded … as a political offence or as an offence connected with a political offence or as an offence inspired by political motives."

The ICJ rules favorably on the "applicability of human rights instruments outside national territory … in the Occupied Palestinian Territory" – quoting time and again other conventions and covenants. These agreements include the International Covenant on Economic, Social and Cultural Rights, the Convention on the Rights of the Child and the Covenant on Civil and Political Rights. All are used as evidence,(with not a single reference to particulars or law), to condemn Israel's abrogation of humanitarian law in building the Barrier against Palestinian terrorists; but the ICJ doesn't so much as mention the "International Convention for the Suppression of Terrorist Bombing." In fact, the term 'suicide bombers' does not appear even once, nor is the "T" word used even once in the wording of the opinion.[117]

---

[116] Ibid.

[117] "Terrorism" appears only five times in the document, cited in brief quotes from the Israeli brief. In the actual ruling, in the name of the ICJ, the word "terrorism" doesn't appear even once.

If General Assembly Resolution 3314[118] and the International Convention for the Suppression of Terrorist Bombings do not make their denunciation of terrorism explicitly clear, resolutions by the Security Council – Resolution 1269[119] adopted in the wake of the first attack on the World Trade Center in 1999 and other resolutions adopted in the wake of the September 11, 2001 terrorist attack on the United States by a non-State terrorist organization – do.

In Point 4 of Security Council Resolution 1269, passed in October 1999 (after the first attack on the World Trade Center), the Security Council calls upon every UN member and non-member:

> "… to take, *inter alia*, in the context of such cooperation and coordination, appropriate steps to:

> "- cooperate with each other, particularly through bilateral and multilateral agreements and arrangements, to prevent and suppress terrorist acts, protect their nationals and other persons against terrorist attacks and bring to justice the perpetrators of such acts."

In essence, the Security Council expects every Member State to carry out this and other steps enumerated in the resolution.

Resolutions 1368,[120] 1373[121] (September 2001) and Resolution 1377[122] (November 2001) leave no room to question Israel's right to defend itself against systematic and sustained Palestinian terrorist attacks launched since September 2000 – an onslaught per capita, equivalent to 17 September 11th attacks.[123]

---

[118] UN General Assembly Resolution 3314 (XXIX). See: http://middleeastfacts.org/content/book/18-aggression-nm-010504.doc. (10495)

[119] UN Security Council, Resolution 1269 Adopted by the Security Council at its 4053rd meeting on 19 October, 1999. See: http://www.un.int/usa/sres1269.htm. (11375)

[120] UN Security Council Resolution 1368 (2001). See: http://www.mefacts.com/cache/pdf/un-resolutions/10574.pdf. (10574)

[121] UN Security Council 1373 (2001) Sep. 28, 2001. (10838)

[122] UN Security Council Resolution 1377 (2001) 12 November 2001. (10837)

[123] Between September 1993 (the signing of the Oslo Accords) and February 2003 (prior to completion of the first leg of the fence) more than 1,004 Israelis lost their lives to Palestinian terrorists.

This document uses extensive links via the Internet. If you experience a broken link, please note the 5 digit number (xxxxx) at the end of the URL and use it as a Keyword in the Search Box at www.MEfacts.com.

With regard to terrorism, Resolution 1368 clarifies and 1373 reconfirms in a broader form that the Security Council

> "*Reaffirms* the inherent right of individual or collective self-defence as recognized by the Charter of the United Nations as reiterated in Resolution 1368 (2001),

> "*Reaffirming* the need to combat by all means, in accordance with the Charter of the United Nations, threats to international peace and security caused by terrorist acts,"

The UN term "by all means" clearly includes a passive, non-lethal physical barrier to impede the movement of such perpetrators, in addition to more *forceful responses.*

Resolution 1377, passed two months later:

> "*Declares* that acts of international terrorism constitute one of the most serious threats to international peace and security in the twenty-first century,

> "*Reaffirms* its unequivocal condemnation of all acts, methods and practices of terrorism as criminal and unjustifiable, regardless of their *motivation,* in all their *forms* and *manifestations, wherever* and by *whomever* committed." [italics by author]

Terrorist attacks - that blow up and destroy public buses, religious celebrations such as a Passover *seder* and bat mitzvah, young people at cafes and discos, families at supermarkets and restaurants, and that murder youth at boarding schools, school outings, and families in their homes and on the road - clearly fall within the confines of this definition. The nature of Palestinian terrorism is public knowledge. Yet the International Court of Justice claims in paragraphs 55-57 of the opinion:

> "According to Israel, if the Court decided to give the requested opinion, it would be forced to speculate about essential facts and make assumptions about arguments of law. More specifically, Israel has argued that the Court could not rule on the legal consequences of the construction of the wall without enquiring, first, into the nature and scope of the security threat to which the wall is intended to respond and the effectiveness of that response, and, second, into the impact of the construction for the Palestinians ... Israel alone possesses much of the necessary information and has stated that it chooses not to address the merits."

Nevertheless, in paragraph 57 of the opinion, the ICJ claims it has ample information:

> "... the Court has at its disposal the report of the Secretary-General,[124] as well as a voluminous dossier submitted by him to the Court. ... The Court notes in particular that Israel's Written Statement, although limited to issues of jurisdiction and judicial propriety, contained observations on other matters, including Israel's concerns in terms of security, and was accompanied by corresponding annexes; many other documents issued by the Israeli Government on those matters are in the public domain."

After all has been said and done,[125] how is it that *nowhere* in the opinion does the ICJ weigh Israel's security threat or even mention terrorism as a factor in the case? The ICJ did not even have to *depend* on Israeli sources. There is, for instance, a well-documented 170-page Human Rights Watch report on suicide bombings against Israelis since September 2000 – *Erased in a Moment: Suicide Bombing Attacks Against Israel Civilians* – available 'in the public domain' at the click of a computer mouse. The report, prepared by a neutral international human rights monitoring organization, concluded: "The scale and systematic nature of these [E.H. terror] attacks in 2001 and 2002 meet the definition of a *crime against humanity*."

Moreover, the Human Rights Watch report, which examines in a special section the justifications given by terrorists for their actions under the right to self-determination, placed responsibility for terrorist acts directly at the Palestinian Authority's door.

Security Council Resolution 1368, passed the day after the September 11th attack, clearly specified who was accountable for such a terrorist act

---

[124] The report includes the following statements: "The Government of Israel has since 1996 considered plans to halt infiltration into Israel from the central and northern West Bank, with the first Cabinet approval of such a plan in July 2001. After a sharp rise in Palestinian terror attacks in the spring of 2002 ..." and "I acknowledge and recognize Israel's right and duty to protect its people against terrorist attacks." See: Report of the Secretary-General prepared pursuant to GA Res. ES-10/13. (10940)

[125] In short, the PA is competent to rule, but if it fails, Israel is to blame for not providing the relevant material ... which the Court in any case rules is immaterial.

This document uses extensive links via the Internet. If you experience a broken link, please note the 5 digit number (xxxxx) at the end of the URL and use it as a Keyword in the Search Box at www.MEfacts.com.

and called for:

> "... bring[ing] to justice the perpetrators, organizers and sponsors of these terrorist attacks and stresses that *those responsible for aiding, supporting or harbouring* the perpetrators, organizers and sponsors of these acts *will be held accountable.*" [italics by author]

The most recent Security Council Resolution 1456 – passed in January 2003 – further clarified:

> "... any acts of terrorism are criminal and unjustifiable, regardless of their motivation, *whenever and by whomsoever committed* and are to be unequivocally condemned, especially when they *indiscriminately target or injure civilians.*"[126] [italics by author]

Again, the International Court of Justice saw no relevance in the definition of terrorism and culpability set forth in this Resolution despite the fact that Israel has been the target of aggression where 80 percent of the Israelis killed were non-combatants, with women and girls accounting for 31 percent of the fatal casualties,[127] including 51 American citizens and a score of foreign laborers.[128]

Another anomaly: The ICJ quotes from a host of international conventions devoted to wartime situations, including the Hague and Geneva Conventions. Is it reasonable that the ICJ was *unaware* of the Rome Statute[129] in force since 2002? It is unlikely. The Statute is clearly posted on the UN International Law website http://www.un.org/law/icc/. What does the Rome Statute say?

In Section IV ("Legal Standards") in the Human Rights Watch (HRW) investigation of suicide bombings, the Rome Statute and the Draft Code

---

[126] UN Security Council Resolution 1456 (2003), [1/20/2003]. (10843)

[127] For a summary of the study see Don Radlauer, "The al-Aqsa Intifada – An Engineered Tragedy," January 7, 2003 at: http://www.ict.org.il/articles/articledet.cfm?articleid=440. For the full study, see http://www.ict.org.il/articles/articledet.cfm?articleid=439.

[128] "Shin Bet report: 1,017 Israelis killed in intifada," *Haaretz*, September 27, 2004. This report also cites 70% of the fatalities (1,017 persons) and 82% of the wounded (5,598 persons) were civilians during four years of violence (September 2000-September 2004).

[129] Israel as well as the United States are not signatories to the Rome Statute.

This document uses extensive links via the Internet. If you experience a broken link, please note the 5 digit number (xxxxx) at the end of the URL and use it as a Keyword in the Search Box at www.MEfacts.com.

Against the Peace and Security of Mankind drawn up by the International Law Commission and often quoted as a guide or yardstick in legal proceedings, albeit not yet formally adopted, are discussed at length.[130] What does the Rome Statute say? The HRW notes:

> "The notion of 'crimes against humanity' refers to acts that, by their scale or nature, outrage the conscience of humankind. Crimes against humanity were first codified in the charter of the Nuremberg Tribunal of 1945. Since then, the concept has been incorporated into a number of international treaties, including the Rome Statute of the International Criminal Court (ICC). Although definitions of crimes against humanity differ slightly from treaty to treaty, all definitions provide that the deliberate, widespread, or systematic killing of civilians by an organization or government is a crime against humanity. Unlike war crimes, crimes against humanity may be committed in times of peace or in periods of unrest that do not rise to the level of an armed conflict."[131]

The most recent definition of crimes against humanity is contained in the Rome Statute of the ICC, which entered into force on July 1, 2002.

> "The statute, in Article 7, defines crimes against humanity as the 'participation in and knowledge of a widespread or systematic attack against a civilian population,' and 'the multiple commission of [such] acts ... against any civilian population, pursuant to or in furtherance of a State or organizational policy to commit such attack.' The statute's introduction defines 'policy to commit such attack' to mean that the state or organization actively promoted or encouraged such attacks against a civilian population. The elements of the 'crime against humanity of murder' require that (1) 'the perpetrator killed one or more persons,' (2) '[t]he conduct was committed as part of a widespread or systematic attack directed against a civilian population,' and (3) '[t]he perpetrator knew that the conduct was part of, or intended the conduct to be part of, a widespread or systematic attack against a civilian population.'"[132]

---

[130] See Section IV, at: http://www.hrw.org/reports/2002/isrl-pa/ISRAELPA1002-04.htm #P564_114276. (11455) See also "Element of Crimes" at the Rome Statute of the International Criminal Court, at: http://www.icc-cpi.int/library/about/officialjournal/basicdocuments/elements(e).pdf. (11456)

[131] See Human Rights Watch at http://www.hrw.org/reports/2002/isrl-pa/ISRAELPA1002-04.htm#P589_123822#P589_123822. (11455)

[132] Ibid.

This document uses extensive links via the Internet. If you experience a broken link, please note the 5 digit number (xxxxx) at the end of the URL and use it as a Keyword in the Search Box at www.MEfacts.com.

It is noteworthy to note that the Rome Statute addresses both the character of the act (deliberate "widespread or systematic" killing), *and* the nature of the perpetrator (a "State" or "organization"), and leaves no loopholes for non-State entities to escape culpability. Yet, the Rome Statute – an integral part of international law – is patently ignored by the International Court of Justice.[133]

Not only UN documents, such as international conventions, are systematically ignored or distorted by the ICJ. So are relevant bilateral treaties, including, the Oslo Accords.

In paragraph 77 of the ICJ opinion, ten years of Palestinian autonomy marked by broken promises to recognize Israel by abolishing anti-Israel clauses in the Palestinian National Covenant and to replace denunciation of terrorism with negotiation, is reduced by the ICJ to *one-sentence*:

> "… a number of agreements have been signed since 1993 between Israel and the Palestine Liberation Organization imposing various obligations on each party."

The ICJ then takes liberties with the content of the Oslo Accords, claiming erroneously:

> "Those agreements *inter alia* required Israel to transfer to Palestinian authorities certain powers and responsibilities exercised in the Occupied Palestinian Territory by its military authorities and civil administration."

In fact, this is a 'doctored' interpretation: Had the members of the ICJ read the Accords, the Bench would have found that Israel only recognized the PLO as the representative of the Palestinian people in the exchange of letters between both sides:

> "In response to your [Arafat] letter of September 9, 1993, I [Yitzhak Rabin, Prime Minister of Israel] wish to inform you that, in light of the PLO

---

[133] See Article 7 (1) (a) Crime against humanity of extermination at: http://www.rk19-biele-feld-mitte.de/info/Recht/United_Nations/Strafgerichtshof/Elements_of_Crime/Article_7.htm#1. (11456)

This document uses extensive links via the Internet. If you experience a broken link, please note the 5 digit number (xxxxx) at the end of the URL and use it as a Keyword in the Search Box at www.MEfacts.com.

commitments included in your letter, the Government of Israel has decided to *recognize the PLO as the representative of the Palestinian people* and commence negotiations with the PLO within the Middle East peace process."[134]

Israel never recognized the claim that the autonomy to be granted Palestinians pertained to 'Occupied Palestinian Territories.' In fact, at no point in the Accords is the West Bank or Gaza labelled 'occupied territory.' The ICJ simply fabricated this and lamely concludes:

> "Such transfers have taken place, but, as a result of subsequent events, they remained partial and limited."

This abridged three-sentence, sanitized the history of the Oslo peace process doesn't so much as hint what "subsequent events" disrupted the peace process – events that have taken the lives of 1366 Israeli victims of terrorism, mostly civilians.[135] Instead, the ICJ claims the only regime is Israeli!

> "... Israel exercises control in the Occupied Palestinian Territory and that, as Israel itself states, the threat which it regards as justifying the construction of the wall originates within, and not outside, that territory."

The ICJ blithely argued with no reference to international law:

> "The situation is thus different from that contemplated by Security Council resolutions 1368 (2001) and 1373 (2001), and therefore Israel could not in any event invoke those resolutions in support of its claim to be exercising a right of self-defence. Consequently, the Court concludes that Article 51 of the Charter has no relevance in this case."

In short, a corrupt 'logic' holds that Israel is solely in charge in a said area, but it is forbidden to take any effective actions in that given area.

The ICJ's 'denial' of Israel's right to act under Resolution 1373 is

---

[134] PLO-Israel Letters of Mutual Recognition. Exchange of Letters between PLO Chairman Yasser Arafat & Israeli Prime Minister Yitzhak Rabin. September 9, 1993. See: http://www.palestine-un.org/peace/p_b.html. (10420)

[135] As of December 3, 2004, and since September 1993, 1,366 Jews have been murdered by Palestinian's terror. For a an updated listing by name see: http://www.masada 2000.org/oslo.html.

This document uses extensive links via the Internet. If you experience a broken link, please note the 5 digit number (xxxxx) at the end of the URL and use it as a Keyword in the Search Box at www.MEfacts.com.

particularly grave. Resolution 1373[136] was adopted by the Security Council under Chapter VII of the UN Charter ("Threats to Peace, Breaches of the Peace and Acts of Aggression.") that invests the Security Council with the power to issue stringent resolutions *requiring all* nations to comply with the terms set forth in Resolution 1373, citing:

> "the need to combat by all means, in accordance with the Charter of the United Nations, threats to international peace and security caused by terrorist acts"

The ICJ has no authority and no power over the Security Council to alter the resolution or wrongly and illegally exclude Israel, a Member State of the UN, from its rights and obligations under Resolution 1373.

Moreover, the ICJ's *position* pretends that a decade of Palestinian autonomy never existed and Palestinians have no margin of control whatsoever over their lives. The threats from suicide bombers and other terrorist acts are magically transformed into an 'internal' problem, so that the Security Council Resolutions passed after September 11th, which allow countries to compromise the sovereignty of other polities to combat terrorism, become inapplicable. Elsewhere in the opinion the ICJ denies Israel the right to take anti-terrorism measures anywhere beyond the Green Line because the same territory 'belongs' to an entity called "Palestine."

Even the British judge on the Bench, Rosalyn Higgins, felt compelled to note in a separate opinion that:

> "Palestine cannot be sufficiently an international entity to be invited to these proceedings, and to benefit from humanitarian law, but not sufficiently an international entity for the prohibition of armed attack on others to be applicable."[137]

Yet this and numerous other reservations did not prevent Higgins from voting in favor of adopting the opinion as written.

---

[136] UN Security Council Resolution 1373 (2001). S/RES/1373 (2001). Adopted by the Security Council at its 4385th meeting, on 28 September 2001. See: http://middleeast facts. org/content/UN-Documents/PDF/SC-res-1373-sep-28-2001.pdf. (10838)

[137] See Judge Higgins at: http://www.icj-cij.org/icjwww/idocket/imwp/imwpframe.htm.

This document uses extensive links via the Internet. If you experience a broken link, please note the 5 digit number (xxxxx) at the end of the URL and use it as a Keyword in the Search Box at www.MEfacts.com.

As far as the ICJ is concerned, Palestinian society lacks any semblance of social organization or self-rule, either on a local or national level, that can be held accountable for terrorism. Yet at the same time, this same Court holds that Palestinians are such a sustainable entity as to deserve *immediate self-determination.*

The ICJ patently ignores the *other* clauses in Oslo II[138] which give the Palestinian Authority full responsibility for Gaza, Jericho and seven major Palestinian cities on the West Bank (Area A), including internal security and public order, a responsibility they abrogated by using control of the civil machinery in 450 towns throughout the West Bank (Area B) to incite the population, including children. It also included turning densely populated areas under full Palestinian control, such as Ramallah and Jenin, into bomb-making factories and staging areas for suicide bombers.

Human Rights Watch – merely a non-governmental organization (NGO) with limited resources equal to or less than those at the disposal of the ICJ – is far more thorough (and fair) in its report on suicide bombings (as mentioned previously in this critique) – *Erased in a Moment.* It doesn't gloss over Palestinian commitments (and complicity) or hide behind the Palestinian Authority's non-state status. It has the courage to say:

> "Although it is not a sovereign state, the Palestinian Authority has explicit security and legal obligations set out in the Oslo Accords, an umbrella term for the series of agreements negotiated between the government of Israel and the PLO from 1993 to 1996. The PA obligations to maintain security and public order were set out in articles XII to XV of the 1995 Interim Agreement on the West Bank and Gaza Strip. These responsibilities were elaborated further in Annex I of the interim agreement, which specifies that the PA will bring to justice those accused of perpetrating attacks against

---

[138] The Israeli-Palestinian Interim Agreement on the West Bank And the Gaza Strip, Washington, D.C. September 28, 1995. Full text see: http://www.mefacts.com/cache/html/oslo/10944.htm. (10944)

This document uses extensive links via the Internet. If you experience a broken link, please note the 5 digit number (xxxxx) at the end of the URL and use it as a Keyword in the Search Box at www.MEfacts.com.

Israeli civilians. According to article II (3)(c) of the annex, the PA will 'apprehend, investigate and prosecute perpetrators and all other persons directly or indirectly involved in acts of terrorism, violence and incitement.'"[139]

These clauses in a landmark international accord, as well as other yardsticks examined by Human Rights Watch in their study and found to be relevant, are of no interest to the International Court of Justice.

The ICJ bases its 'conclusion' on General Assembly Resolution 58/163 that "reaffirms the right of the Palestinian people ... to their independent State of Palestine."[140] The General Assembly, of course, has no authorization to 'hand out' polities like lollipops any more than the ICJ has the right to give this bogus right a legal 'stamp of approval' because neither body has actual legislative or executive powers.

Under the Law of Nations, rights go hand-in-hand with responsibilities. Entitlement is irrevocably tied to accountability. The entire opinion penned by the International Court of Justice speaks time and again of Palestinian rights, but *not once* about Palestinians' commitments. If Palestinians are unable to behave in a manner in keeping with the most fundamental principles of the Law of Nations – attacking their neighbors as opposed to peaceful negotiation of differences – then surely Israel has the right to defend such an onslaught of its national security. But alas, the entire issue of terrorism is considered immaterial to the security barrier question, which the ICJ brands a political ploy that merely grabs Palestinian land and abridges Palestinians' rights.

---

[139] HUMAN RIGHTS WATCH. "Erased In A Moment: Suicide Bombing Attacks Against Israeli Civilians," October 2002. Obligations of the Palestinian Authority and Armed Palestinian Groups, at: http://www.hrw.org/reports/2002/isrl-pa/ISRAELPA1002-04.htm#TopOfPage. (11262)

[140] UN General Assembly - 58/163. A/RES/58/163. 77th plenary meeting. 22 December 2003. The right of the Palestinian people to self-determination. See: http://domino.un.org/UNISPAL.NSF/0/e5eaf52d1c576d0785256e6d0055b152?OpenDocument. (11319)

This document uses extensive links via the Internet. If you experience a broken link, please note the 5 digit number (xxxxx) at the end of the URL and use it as a Keyword in the Search Box at www.MEfacts.com.

Report of the UN High-level Panel on Threats, Challenges and Change.

On 2 December 2004, the UN Secretary-General released a report entitled "A more secure world: Our shared responsibility."

This report, more than one year in the making, deals with the global treats of terrorism, and clearly contradicts the ICJ's Advisory Opinion on some of the core issues regarding terrorism and self-defence, stating that the:

> "biggest security threats we face now, and in the decades ahead, go far beyond States waging aggressive war. They extend to ... terrorism; . ... The threats are *from non-State actors* [E.H. such as the Palestinians] as well as States [E.H. such as Syria, Saudi Arabia, Iran], and to human security as well as State security." [italics by author]

The report continues to challenge the Court assertion that Resolution 1373 is not applicable to Israel [E.H. as the court did without reference to law, or other supportive source] by stating:

> "Security Council resolution 1373 (2001) imposed uniform, mandatory counter-terrorist obligations on *all States* ..." [italics by author]

It proceeds to explain that the respond to the use of force by non-State has been inadequate:

> "159. The norms governing the use of force by non-State actors have not kept pace with those pertaining to States. ... Legally, virtually all forms of terrorism are prohibited by one of 12 international counter-terrorism conventions, international customary law, the Geneva Conventions or the Rome Statutes. Legal scholars know this [E.H. which the ICJ seems to ignore] ... The United Nations must achieve the same degree of normative strength concerning non-State use of force as it has concerning State use of force." And that "... there is *nothing* in the fact of occupation that justifies the targeting and killing of civilians. [italics by author]

> "161. ... Attacks that specifically target innocent civilians and non-combatants must be condemned clearly and unequivocally by all."

One would hope that logic, fairness and international law 'as is' will lead the UN General Assembly to follow the suggestions and recommendations of this report, leaving behind the biased Advisory Opinion of the International Court of Justice.

7 Self-defence – Legitimate Use of Force

UN Charter Article 51 is not the only UN sanction of self-defence disregarded or overlooked by the ICJ.[141] The Court chooses to totally ignore a number of highly-relevant United Nations Resolutions, passed by both the General Assembly and the Security Council, addressing the legitimate use of force in self-defence by Member States.

For instance: the rationale behind General Assembly Resolution 3314 "Definition of Aggression" is highly relevant to the case at hand. It states:

> "*Convinced* that the adoption of a definition of aggression ought to have the effect of deterring a potential aggressor, would simplify the determination of acts of aggression and the implementation of measures to suppress them and would also facilitate the protection of the rights and lawful interests of, and the rendering of assistance to, the victim, ..."[142]

---

[141] Article 51 reads: "Nothing in the present Charter shall impair the inherent right of individual or collective self-defence if an armed attack occurs against a Member of the United Nations, until the Security Council has taken measures necessary to maintain international peace and security. Measures taken by Members in the exercise of this right of self-defence shall be immediately reported to the Security Council and shall not in any way affect the authority and responsibility of the Security Council under the present Charter to take at any time such action as it deems necessary in order to maintain or restore international peace and security." See: http://www.un.org/aboutun/charter/chapter7.htm. (10370)

[142] UN General Assembly Resolution 3314 (XXIX). http://middleeastfacts.org/content/book/18-aggression-nm-010504.doc. (10495)

This document uses extensive links via the Internet. If you experience a broken link, please note the 5 digit number (xxxxx) at the end of the URL and use it as a Keyword in the Search Box at www.MEfacts.com.

The ICJ speaks repeatedly of the "inadmissibility of the acquisition of territory by war." What does this phrase mean in the framework of international law? The ICJ's use of this important principle is selective, misplaced, misleading and totally out of context.

The Bench chooses to quote Article 2, paragraph 4, of the UN Charter, which says:

> "All Members shall refrain in their international relations from the threat or use of force against the territorial integrity or political independence of any State, or in any other manner inconsistent with the Purposes of the United Nations."

But the Bench chooses to ignore Article 5, paragraph 3, of UN GA Resolution 3314 which states:

> "No territorial acquisition or special advantage *resulting from aggression* is or shall be recognized as lawful." [italics by author]

That is, the inadmissibility of the acquisition of territory by war cannot and should not be viewed as a blanket statement. Rather, it hinges on acquisition being the result of aggression. Arab countries acted aggressively against Israel in 1948 and 1967. Israel was not the aggressor, neither in Israel's 1948 War of Independence nor in the 1967 Six-Day War.

In the same deceptive manner, the ICJ quotes selectively from the 1970 General Assembly Resolution 2625[143] ("Declaration on Principles of International Law Concerning Friendly Relations and Co-operation Among States"). In paragraph 87 of the ICJ opinion, the Bench notes that Resolution 2625:

> "… emphasized that 'No territorial acquisition resulting from the threat or use of force shall be recognized as legal.'"

It hides from the reader that the same Resolution subsequently clarifies that:

---

[143] "Declaration on principles of international law concerning friendly relations and cooperation among states in accordance with the charter of the united nations" at: http://www.un.org/documents/ga/res/25/ares25.htm. (11029)

This document uses extensive links via the Internet. If you experience a broken link, please note the 5 digit number (xxxxx) at the end of the URL and use it as a Keyword in the Search Box at www.MEfacts.com.

"The territory of a State shall not be the object of military occupation *resulting from* the use of force in contravention of the provisions of the Charter." [italics by author]

And the same Resolution continues:

"Nothing in the foregoing paragraphs shall be construed as enlarging or diminishing in any way the scope of the provisions of the Charter concerning *cases in which the use of force is lawful*." [italics by author]

Professor, Judge Schwebel explains that the principle of "acquisition of territory by war is inadmissible" must be read together with other principles:

"… namely, that no legal right shall spring from a wrong, and the Charter principle that the Members of the United Nations shall refrain in their international relations from the threat or use of force against the territorial integrity or political independence of any State." [144]

Simply stated: Arab illegal aggression against the territorial integrity and political independence of Israel, can not be reworded.

Had the Charter forbidden use of force in any and all manners and situations, it would not need to use the words "resulting from." The Resolution would have simply read: "The territory of a State shall not be the object of military occupation by another State." Period.

It is relevant at this juncture to recall again Judge, Sir Elihu Lauterpacht's explanation on this important issue (a point which was also cited by Judge Schwebel in his writings):

"… territorial change cannot properly take place as a result of the 'unlawful' use of force. But to omit the word 'unlawful' is to change the substantive content of the rule and to turn an important safeguard of legal principle into an aggressor's charter. For if force can never be used to effect lawful territory change, then, if territory has once changed hands as a result of the unlawful use of force, the illegitimacy of the position thus established is sterilized by the prohibition upon the use of force to restore the lawful sovereign. This cannot be regarded as reasonable or correct." [145]

---

[144] Professor, Judge Schwebel in *What Weight to Conquest?* in "Justice in International Law," Cambridge University Press, 1994.

[145] Professor, Judge Sir Elihu Lauterpacht, "Jerusalem and the Holy Places," Pamphlet No. 19 (London, Anglo-Israel Association, 1968)·

That is, there are situations involving *lawful* use of force and there are *lawful* occupations in the course of repelling aggression. Article 51 addresses the right to self-defence and the lawful use of force when one faces an aggressor.

The Security Council is the only UN body authorized to label a Member State (or non-State entity) an aggressor. In the Preamble of Resolution 3314 ('Definition of Aggression') it says:

> "Recalling that the Security Council, in accordance with Article 39 of the Charter of the United Nations, shall determine the existence of any threat to the peace, breach of the peace or act of aggression and shall make recommendations, or decide what measures shall be taken in accordance with Articles 41 and 42, to maintain or restore international peace and security."[146]

Who is labeled aggressor?

The Security Council has never labeled Israel an aggressor in its entire history. Attempts by the International Court of Justice to misuse the slogan "inadmissibility of the acquisition of territory by war" concerning Israel, in a case that it patently refuses to recognize has a strong security component, is simply disgraceful.

General Assembly Resolution 3314 makes it adamantly clear that no group, including non-State entities, individuals or groups, can expect to be shielded behind such a narrow and warped interpretation of Article 51 (the right to Self-Defence). Passed unanimously in 1974 without even a formal vote, Article 3(a) clarifies that the definition of a State when defining aggressors must be loosely construed:

> "… without prejudice to questions of recognition or to whether a State is a member of the United Nations."[147]

---

[146] See discussion in this critique, Chapter 8: "Attempting to Brand Israel the Aggressor."

[147] UN General Assembly Resolution 3314 (XXIX) at: http://middleeastfacts.org/content/book/18-aggression-nm-010504.doc (10495)

This document uses extensive links via the Internet. If you experience a broken link, please note the 5 digit number (xxxxx) at the end of the URL and use it as a Keyword in the Search Box at www.MEfacts.com.

This clause clearly covers aggression emanating from the Palestinian Authority, an internationally recognized autonomous, national political entity established by international treaty – the Oslo Accords.[148] Moreover, Article 3(g) cites specifically that this includes:

> "… the sending by or on behalf of a State of armed hands, groups, irregulars or mercenaries, which carry out acts of armed force against another State of such gravity as to amount to the acts listed above, or its substantial involvement therein."

Furthermore, in Article 4, Resolution 3314 notes that "… the acts enumerated above are not exhaustive" and declares they can be further enumerated by the Security Council. Palestinian terrorist organizations, with headquarters and support in places such as Gaza, Jenin, Lebanon, Iran and Syria, using areas under the civil and security responsibility of the Palestinian Authority as organizational and staging areas to commit terrorist acts, clearly fall within the confines of this Resolution. Resolution 3314 defines aggression in Article 3(b), in a list of acts of aggression, as

> "… the use of any weapons by a State against the territory of another State."

This clause clearly covers the waves of suicide bombers targeting Israeli civilians . Either the ICJ pretends this resolution doesn't exist or it is so incompetent that it doesn't know the resolution exists.

'Whomever' means – Anyone!

The ICJ's attempt to qualify the use of self-defence under Article 51 as aggression committed by 'state' only, is clearly an attempt to evade International law and Security Council Resolutions that *require* fighting terrorism by *whomever committed* – No escape clause … *whomever* means *anyone*!

---

[148] See: Israel-PLO Agreement: Oslo, 1993 [9/13/1993] Ref #11318. (11318) and Oslo II Interim Agreement - Washington, D.C., September 28, 1995 [9/28/1995] Ref #10944. (10944)

Security Council Resolution 1269[149] – in the wake of the first attack on the World Trade Center (in 1999); Resolution 1373 (September 2001) and Resolution 1377 (November 2001) – after the September 11 attacks; and Security Council Resolution 1456 (January 2003) all deplore terrorism and censure its use in any case or form "*regardless of their motivation, whenever and by whomever committed.*" The same language appears in the only convention in international law dealing with terrorism, Resolution 52/164 – the *International Convention for the Suppression of Terrorist Bombings.*[150]

All of these documents, that underscore repeatedly that terrorism must be fought by *all parties*, by *all means*, at *all times*, against *all perpetrators*, are detailed elsewhere in this critique; but not one is cited by the ICJ – not in its discussion of Article 51 and the right of a Member State to self-defence nor in any other context within the ICJ's opinion.

Even Kofi Annan had the integrity to declare in an October 2001 address before the General Assembly meeting, called to discuss terrorism in the wake of September 11th, that "the greatest immediate danger arises from a *non-state group* – or even an *individual.*"[151] The ICJ simply puts on blinders that black out reality.

The ICJ didn't even give these documents, that arguably support Israel's right to erect a non-lethal barrier against terrorists in self-defence (directed and permitted to do even a lot more), the respect of a discussion.

---

[149] UN Security Council, Resolution 1269 Adopted by the Security Council at its 4053rd meeting on 19 October, 1999. See: http://www.mefacts.com/cache/html/un-resolutions/11375.htm. (11375)

[150] UN General Assembly, International Convention for the Suppression of Terrorist Bombings, Adopted without a vote, 15 December 1997. See: http://www.un.org/ga/documents/gares52/res52164.htm. (10899)

[151] The Secretary-General Address to the General Assembly on Terrorism, New York, 1 October, 2001. "Mr. President, [Mayor Giuliani,]: ... While the world was unable to prevent the 11 September attacks, there is much we can do to help prevent future terrorist acts carried out with weapons of mass destruction. The greatest immediate danger arises from a non-state group — or even an individual ..." See: http://www.escwa.org.lb/information/press/un/2001/1oct.html. (10847)

8 Attempting to Brand Israel the Aggressor

Using provocative words such as "Belligerents" (In paragraph 84), "Belligerency" (In paragraph 89) and "Hostile" (In paragraph 78 of the opinion), the ICJ's opinion attempts to deliver the impression that Israel is an "aggressor" who deserves no rights.[152]

In 1974, the United Nations General Assembly adopted a definition of "aggression" in the context of establishing international peace when it approved Resolution 3314.[153] The resolution reaffirms the principles of the UN Charter and the Declaration on Principles of International Law, which states that "… war of aggression constitutes a crime against the peace, for which there is responsibility under international law."

When applied to major battles between Israel and the Arab states in 1948, 1956, 1967 and 1973 and the continuing fight of self-defence against Palestinian Arab terrorism, the UN's 1974 definition of aggression clearly and unequivocally would label the Arab states and the

---

[152] UN General Assembly Resolution 3314 (XXIX). Definition of Aggression, 14 December, 1974 see: http://middleeastfacts.org/content/book/18-aggression-nm-010504.doc. (10495)

[153] Ibid.

This document uses extensive links via the Internet. If you experience a broken link, please note the 5 digit number (xxxxx) at the end of the URL and use it as a Keyword in the Search Box at www.MEfacts.com.

Arab Palestinians as the aggressors in both their direct and indirect acts of hostility against Israel.[154]

The following comments in regard to certain paragraphs of Resolution 3314, demonstrate just who is the aggressor in the Arab-Israeli conflict under International Laws.

1. Article 1 defines "aggression" as the use of armed force against the sovereignty, territorial integrity or political independence of a State. An "Explanatory note:" follows to explains that "In this Definition the term 'State'":

"(a) is used without prejudice to questions of recognition or to whether a State is a member of the United Nations;" which means to say that acts of aggression applies [apply] also to "people," State [refers]not [only to] members of the UN, or other non-recognized States. This note is given to understand that *aggression* can apply to *any* aggressor including the Arab Palestinians or the Palestinian Authority.

2. Article 2, 25 years after the fact, establishes that the Arab states that attacked the newly declared State of Israel in 1948 (known as the Israel War of Independence) were all aggressors.

Also, in 1967 during the Six-Day War, Jordan,[155] who joined Egypt and initiated 'the first use of armed forces' against Israel, was clearly the aggressors.

---

[154] Professor, Judge Stephen M. Schwebel, *What Weight to Conquest?* in "Justice in International Law", Cambridge University Press, 1994. "As between Israel, acting defensively in 1948 and 1967, on the one hand, and her Arab neighbors, acting aggressively in 1948 and 1967, on the other, Israel has better title in the territory of what was Palestine, including the whole of Jerusalem."

[155] "In response to the Israeli attack [on Egypt], Jordanian forces launched an offensive into Israel, but were soon driven back as the Israeli forces counterattacked into the West Bank and Arab East Jerusalem." From the official website of Jordan at: http://www.mefacts.com/cache/html/jordan/10364.htm. (10364)

3. Article 3 (c) – In both 1956 and 1967, Egypt blockaded the Strait of Tiran, preventing access to Israel's southern port of Eilat, a hostile action that led to the Sinai Campaign in 1956 and to the Six-Day War in 1967. As defined by the UN's 1974 resolution, Egypt indisputably committed an acts of aggression.

Article 3 (f) – Lebanon's acquiescence, in allowing Syrian armed forces to use Lebanon as a platform to wage war against Israel by supporting Hezbollah's terrorist attacks, clearly puts Lebanon in the category of aggressor by 'lending' its territory to the Syrians.

Article 3 (g) – Under this Article, Lebanon, Syria and Iran are clearly aggressors. By allowing Hezbollah to freely launch attacks from its territory, Lebanon permits armed aggression against Israel. Syria and Iran are aggressors as they are clearly Hezbollah's greatest supporters in the region.

Article 6 – Applies when a use of force is exercised under the UN Charter's definition of self-defence and in cases in which the use of force is *lawful*.[156]

Israel's enemies unsuccessful in branding Israel the aggressor.

UN Draft resolutions attempting to brand Israel as aggressor or illegal occupier as a result of the 1967 Six-Day War, were all defeated by either the UN General Assembly or the Security Council:

---

[156] "Nothing in the foregoing paragraphs shall be construed as enlarging or diminishing in any way the scope of the provisions of the Charter concerning cases in which the *use of force is lawful*." [italics by author], General Assembly Resolution 2625, "Declaration on Principles of International Law Concerning Friendly Relations and Co-operation Among States." See: UN GA Res. 2625 (XXV) 24 October 1970 at http://www.un.org/documents/ga/res/25/ares25.htm. (11029)

This document uses extensive links via the Internet. If you experience a broken link, please note the 5 digit number (xxxxx) at the end of the URL and use it as a Keyword in the Search Box at www.MEfacts.com.

A/L.519,[157] 19 June 1967, submitted by: the Union of Soviet Socialist Republics, "Israel, in gross violation of the Charter of the United Nations and the universally accepted principles of international law, has committed a premeditated and previously prepared aggression against the United Arab Republic, Syria and Jordan ..."

A/L.521,[158] 26 June 1967, submitted by: Albania "Resolutely condemns the Government of Israel for its armed aggression against the United Arab Republic, the Syrian Arab Republic and Jordan, and for the continuance of the aggression by keeping under its occupation parts of the territory of these countries."

A/L.522/REV.3*,[159] 3 July 1967, submitted by: Afghanistan, Burundi, Cambodia, Ceylon, Congo (Brazzaville), Cyprus, Guinea, India, Indonesia, Malaysia, Mali, Pakistan, Senegal, Somalia, United Republic of Tanzania, Yugoslavia and Zambia. "Calls upon Israel to withdraw immediately all its forces to the positions they held prior to 5 June 1967."

A/L.523/Rev.1,[160] 4 July 1967, submitted by: Argentina, Barbados, Bolivia, Brazil, Chile, Colombia, Costa Rica, Dominican Republic, Ecuador, El Salvador, Guatemala, Guyana, onduras, Jamaica, Mexico, Nicaragua, Panama, Paraguay, Trinidad and Tobago and Venezuela. "Israel to withdraw all its forces from all the territories occupied by it as a result of the recent conflict; ..."

---

[157] Union of Soviet Socialist Republics: draft resolution, A/L.519, 19 June 1967, DOCUMENT A/L.519 at: http://domino.un.org/unispal.nsf/0/2795fff6b5 8b212c052566cd006e0900?OpenDocument. (10919)

[158] Draft Resolution A/L. 521, by Albania at the Emergency Session of the General Assembly- 26 June 1967, see: http://www.mefacts.com/cache/html/un-resolutions/10921.htm. (10921)

[159] Document A/L.522/REV.3*, 3 July 1967, Afghanistan, Burundi, Cambodia, Ceylon, Congo (Brazzaville), Cyprus, Guinea, India, Indonesia, Malaysia, Mali, Pakistan, Senegal, Somalia, United Republic of Tanzania, Yugoslavia and Zambia: Revised draft resolution. (10918)

[160] A/L.523/Rev.1, 4 July 1967, Fifth emergency special session Agenda item 5. Argentina, Barbados, Bolivia, Brazil, Chile, Colombia, Costa Rica, Dominican Republic, Ecuador, El Salvador, Guatemala, Guyana, Honduras, Jamaica, Mexico, Nicaragua, Panama, Paraguay, Trinidad and Tobago and Venezuela: revised draft resolution. See: http://domino.un.org/UNISPAL.NSF/0/510ef41fac855100052566cd00750ca4?OpenDo cument. (10920)

This document uses extensive links via the Internet. If you experience a broken link, please note the 5 digit number (xxxxx) at the end of the URL and use it as a Keyword in the Search Box at www.MEfacts.com.

9 UN Security Council Resolutions 242 and 338

The United Nations Security Council never branded Israel as an "Unlawful Occupier" or an "Aggressor" and never called on Israel to withdraw from *all* the "Territories."

The wording of UN Resolutions 242[161] and 338[162] clearly reflects the contention that none of the Territories were occupied territories taken by force in an *unjust war*.

Because the Arabs were clearly the aggressors, nowhere in UN Security Council Resolutions 242 or 338 – the cornerstones of a peace settlement – is Israel branded as an *invader or unlawful occupier* of the Territories.

The minutes of the six month 'debate' over the wording of Resolution 242, as noted in the close of Chapter 8, show that draft resolution proposals were presented that speak of "occupied territories", "aggression" and which called on Israel to "withdraw immediately all its forces to the positions they held prior to 5 June 1967," however, were all defeated.

---

[161] UN Security Council resolution 242 (1967) of 22 November 1967. See: ttp://domino.un.org/UNISPAL.NSF/0/7d35e1f729df491c85256ee700686136?OpenDocument. (10065)

[162] UN Security Council resolution 338 (1973) of 22 October 1973. See: http://www.mefacts.com/cache/html/un-documents/10066.htm. (10066)

This document uses extensive links via the Internet. If you experience a broken link, please note the 5 digit number (xxxxx) at the end of the URL and use it as a Keyword in the Search Box at www.MEfacts.com.

Professor Eugene V. Rostow went on record in 1991 to make this clear:

> "Resolution 242, which as Undersecretary of State of Political Affairs between 1966 and 1969, I helped to produce, calls on the parties to make peace and *allows Israel to administer the territories it occupied in 1967* until 'a just and lasting peace in the Middle East' is achieved. ... Speaker after speaker made it explicit that Israel was not to be forced back to the 'fragile' and 'vulnerable' Armistice Demarcation Lines, but should retire once peace was made to what Resolution 242 called 'secure and recognized' boundaries, agreed upon by the parties."[163] [italics by author]

Former British Ambassador to the UN, Lord Caradon, the principal author of the Resolution 242 draft, indicated the same in a 1974 statement in which he said:

> "It would have been wrong to demand that Israel return to its positions of 4 June 1967. ... That's why we didn't demand that the Israelis return to them and I think we were right not to."[164]

Arthur J. Goldberg,[165] the U.S. Ambassador to the UN in 1967 and a key draftee of Resolution 242, stated:

> "The notable omissions in language used to refer to withdrawal are the words *the, all,* and the *June 5, 1967, lines.* I refer to the English text of the resolution. The French and Soviet texts differ from the English in this respect, but the English text was voted on by the Security Council, and thus it is determinative. In other words, there is lacking a declaration requiring Israel to withdraw from the (or all the) territories occupied by it on and after

---

[163] Eugene V. Rostow, "The Future of Palestine," Institute for National Strategic Studies, November 1993. Professor Rostow was Sterling Professor of Law and Public Affairs Emeritus at Yale University and served as the Dean of Yale Law School (1955-66); Distinguished Research Professor of Law and Diplomacy, National Defense University; Adjunct Fellow, American Enterprise Institute. In 1967 as U.S. Under-Secretary of State for Political Affairs he become a key draftee of the UN Resolution 242.

[164] Lord Caradon (Sir Hugh Foot) was the UK representative to the UN in 1967. His final draft becomes the foundation for UN Resolution 242. See Beirut Daily Star, 12 June 1974, as quoted by Leonard J. Davis in Myths and Facts (Washington: Near East Report, 1989), p. 48, cited in Dan Diker, "Does the International News Media Overlook Israel's Legal Rights in the Palestinian-Israeli Conflict," JCPA, at: http://www.jcpa.org/jl/vp495.htm.

[165] Goldberg, Arthur, was a professor of law at the John Marshall Law School in Chicago. Appointed in 1962 to the U.S. Supreme Court. In 1965 he was appointed U.S. representative to the United Nations. Judge Goldberg was a key draftee of UN Resolution 242.

June 5, 1967. Instead, the resolution stipulates *withdrawal from occupied territories without defining the extent of withdrawal.* And it can be inferred from the incorporation of the words *secure and recognized boundaries* that the territorial adjustments to be made by the parties in their peace settlements could encompass less than a complete withdrawal of Israeli forces from occupied territories."[166] [italics by author]

Political figures and international jurists have discussed the existence of "permissible" or "legal occupations." In a seminal article on this question, entitled *What Weight to Conquest,* Professor Schwebel, a former president of the International Court of Justice, wrote:

"... a state [E.H. Israel] acting in lawful exercise of its right of self-defense may seize and occupy foreign territory as long as such seizure and occupation are necessary to its self-defense; (c) where the prior holder of territory had seized that territory unlawfully, the state which subsequently takes that territory in the lawful exercise of self-defense has, against that prior holder, *better title.*

"... as between Israel, acting defensively in 1948 and 1967, on the one hand, and her Arab neighbors, acting aggressively, in 1948 and 1967, on the other, Israel has the better title in the territory of what was Palestine, including the *whole of Jerusalem,* than do Jordan and Egypt."[167] [italics by author]

Professor Julius Stone, a leading authority on the Law of Nations, has concurred, further clarifying:

"Territorial Rights Under International Law. ... By their [Arab countries] armed attacks against the State of Israel in 1948, 1967, and 1973, and by various acts of belligerency throughout this period, these Arab states flouted their basic obligations as United Nations members to refrain from threat or use of force against Israel's territorial integrity and political independence. These acts were in flagrant violation *inter alia* of Article 2(4) and paragraphs (1), (2), and (3) of the same article."[168]

---

[166] Goldberg, "U.N. Resolution 242: Origin, Meaning, and Significance." National Committee on American Foreign Policy. See article at: http://www.mefacts.com/cache/html/arab-countries/10159.htm. (10159)

[167] Professor, Judge Stephen M. Schwebel, *What Weight to Conquest?* in "Justice in International Law", Cambridge University Press, 1994. Opinions quoted in this critiques are not derived from his position as a judge of the ICJ.

[168] Professor Julius Stone, "Israel and Palestine, Assault on the Law of Nations" The Johns Hopkins University Press, 1981.

This document uses extensive links via the Internet. If you experience a broken link, please note the 5 digit number (xxxxx) at the end of the URL and use it as a Keyword in the Search Box at www.MEfacts.com.

One *must* note that none of the writing and opinions of these authoritative, respected and reliable sources are considered by the ICJ, although in stark contrast, the "legal position of the Palestinian Liberation Organization" is noted. The PLO position, that "the wall severs the territorial sphere over which the Palestinian people are entitled to exercise their right of self-determination and constitutes a violation of the legal principle prohibiting the acquisition of territory by the use of force" – is carefully noted and addressed in paragraph 115 of the ICJ's opinion.

10 Territories – Legality of Jewish Settlements

The ICJ not only purports to have *all* the necessary information to give an advisory opinion on the legality of the fence but also went beyond its own mandate from the General Assembly – in apparent eagerness to 'do its master's bidding' without being asked to do so, advising that Jewish settlements are illegal. In paragraph 120 of the Court's opinion, the ICJ declares:

> "The Court concludes that the Israeli settlements in the Occupied Palestinian Territory (including East Jerusalem) have been established in breach of international law."

The ICJ based its conclusion on the inappropriate use of an article of the Fourth Geneva Convention which stipulates:

> "The Occupying Power shall not deport or transfer parts of its own civilian population into the territory it occupies,"

coupled with a host of anti-Israeli UN General Assembly resolutions passed in the 1990s that describe the West Bank and Gaza as "Palestinian Occupied Territories" and declare Israeli settlements – including hundreds of thousands of Jewish Jerusalemites living in numerous new neighborhoods built since 1967 – to be illegal settlers.

For example, in paragraph 19 of the opinion, the ICJ notes that in 1997 the Security Council *rejected* two one-sided draft resolutions that *sought* to brand Israeli settlements as *illegal* (draft S/1997/199,[169] SC S/PV.3747 and draft S/1997/241,[170] SC S/PV.3756).[171] The ICJ then proceeds to solemnly quote a resolution subsequently passed by the General Assembly (not the Security Council) (Resolution ES-10/2). The Bench underscores in paragraph 19, that:

> "... the General Assembly expressed its conviction that: 'the repeated violation by Israel, the occupying Power, of international law' and condemned the 'illegal Israeli actions' in occupied East Jerusalem and the rest of the Occupied Palestinian Territory, in particular the construction of settlements in that territory."

One is led to believe that, because the 'automatic' majority of Members of the United Nations ... concurred with bringing the subject of so-called "illegal Israeli actions in occupied East Jerusalem and the rest of the Occupied Palestinian Territory" to the Assembly and voted on it, this UN citation makes the document true and relevant from a legal standpoint. One is led to believe that repeating such *sentiments* eleven times (all duly cited for the record by the Bench) makes the UN document admissible as the basis for establishing the legality or illegality of an action in the international court of law.

The ICJ seems to take at face value the wording of the General Assembly request for the ICJ to give an advisory opinion, without checking its accuracy or legal standing. The General Assembly request reads:

> "*Recalling in particular* relevant United Nations resolutions affirming that Israeli settlements in the Occupied Palestinian Territory, including East

---

[169] Rejected - UN Security Council draft resolution S/1997/199, 7 March 1997. See: http://domino.un.org/UNISPAL.NSF/0/f97c162f6a30647205256531005b4e15?OpenDocument. (11379)

[170] Draft SC Resolution (res no. S/S/1997/241) Vetoed by the U.S. 21 March 1997. See: http://domino.un.org/UNISPAL.NSF/0/88f7fb474668764705256531005b7239?OpenDocument. (11380)

[171] The fact that the Security Council rejected these resolutions in recent years is highly significant in another context: It is a reaffirmation, in the negative, that the Security Council continues to viewed the West Bank as disputed territory whose future and borders must be settled by the parties as the Security Council declared in 1967 (Resolution 242) and 1973 (Resolution 338).

Jerusalem, are illegal and an obstacle to peace and to economic and social development as well as those demanding the complete cessation of settlement activities."[172]

The limited powers of the General Assembly.

As incredulous as it may be, the ICJ seems ignorant of the General Assembly's powers or perhaps prefers to ignore them. The judges even fail to note that "affirmation" means merely a declarative statement of *sentiment*. It is not a directive. It is not law. In any case, this and a host of other anti-Israel resolutions passed annually are not legally binding documents by any measure. One need only to read the UN Charter to establish this fact. Article 10 of the UN Charter states:

> "The General Assembly may *discuss* any questions or any matters within the scope of the present Charter or relating to the powers and functions of any organs provided for in the present Charter, and, except as provided in Article 12, *may make recommendations* to the Members of the United Nations or to the Security Council or to both on any such questions or matters." [italics by author]

Past members of the Bench have gone on record to emphsize that the UN Charter does not grant the General Assembly (or the International Court of Justice, for that matter) authority to enact or amend international law.

Professor Judge Schwebel, former President of the International Court of Justice (1997-2000), has stated that:

> "… the General Assembly of the United Nations can only, in principle, issue 'recommendation' which are not of a binding character, according to Article 10 of the Charter of the United Nations."

---

[172] United Nations, General Assembly Resolution, A/RES/ES-10/14, "Illegal Israeli actions in Occupied East Jerusalem and the rest of the Occupied Palestinian Territory" 12 December 2003. See: http://middleeastfacts.org/content/UN-Documents/A-RES-ES-10-14.htm. (10938)

This document uses extensive links via the Internet. If you experience a broken link, please note the 5 digit number (xxxxx) at the end of the URL and use it as a Keyword in the Search Box at www.MEfacts.com.

Schwebel also cites the (1950) opinion of Judge, Sir Hersch Lauterpacht, a former member judge of the International Court of Justice, who declared that:

> "… the General Assembly has no legal power to legislate or bind its members by way of recommendation."

Yet another former ICJ judge, Sir Gerald Fitzmaurice has been just as resolved in rejecting what he labeled the "illusion" that a General Assembly resolution can have "legislative effect."[173]

Academics and renowned international law experts also agree. Professor Stone illuminates this subject by pointing out:

> "In his book The Normative Role of the General Assembly of the United Nations and the Declaration of Principles of Friendly Relations, Professor Gaetano Arangio-Ruiz[174] is led to conclude that the General Assembly lacks legal authority either to enact or to 'declare' or 'determine' or 'interpret' international law so as legally to bind states by such acts, whether these states be members of the United Nations or not, and whether these states voted for or against or abstained from the relevant vote or did not take part in it."[175, 176]

The Territories and the war of words.

One can easily trace the General Assembly's attempts to *legislate* changes in the status of the Territories. How the definition of the status of the Territories was 'doctored' is well documented on the website of the Palestinian delegation to the United Nations that posts landmark pro-Palestinian decisions. Examination reveals how over the years UN

---

173 Cited in "Israel and Palestine, Assault on the law of nations," Professor Julius Stone, The Johns Hopkins University Press, 1981. p. 29.

174 Professor Gaetano Arangio-Ruiz "The United Nations declaration on friendly relations and the system of the sources of international law" Publisher: Alphen aan den Rijn, The Netherlands; Germantown, Md.: Sijthoff & Noordhoff, 1979. ISBN: 902860149X.

175 Ibid, p. 40. Professor Julius Stone – another eminent scholar of international law – labeled Ruiz's work "perhaps the most comprehensive and up-to-date treatise on this matter".

176 See the Hague Academy of International Law, at: http://www.ppl.nl/bibliographies/all/showresults.php?bibliography=recueil&keyword1ppn=076252078&keyword=General%20Assembly.

General Assembly resolutions and the wording of resolutions by sub-committees moves from "territories" to "occupied territories" to "Occupied Territories" and "Arab territories" to "occupied Palestinian territories" to "Occupied Palestinian Territory" and "occupied Palestinian territory, including Jerusalem":

• Resolution 3236 (XXIX)[177] passed in November 1974 speaks of "the question of Palestine";

• Resolution 38/58[178] in December 1983 speaks of "Arab territories" and "occupied territories";

• Resolution 43/176[179] passed in December 1988 expresses sentiments suggesting Palestinian entitlement – speaking of "the Palestinian people['s] right to exercise their sovereignty over their territory occupied since 1967";

• Resolution 51/133[180] passed in December 1996 adds Jerusalem in particular – speaking of "occupied Palestinian territory, including Jerusalem, and the occupied Syrian Golan";

• Resolution 52/250[181] passed in July 1998 fully "assigns title" – speaking of "Occupied Palestinian Territory," a designation that is frequently used in subsequent resolutions.

None of these terms have a legal foundation any more than declaring "The world is flat" makes it so. Yet the International Court of Justice cites these terms as if they were *legal* documents, all in violation of the Court's Statute.

---

[177] See: http://domino.un.org/UNISPAL.NSF/0/025974039acfb171852560de00548bbe? OpenDocument. (11382)

[178] See: http://domino.un.org/UNISPAL.NSF/0/2fdd47753d2ae353852560d8006ca36b? OpenDocument. (11383)

[179] See: http://domino.un.org/UNISPAL.NSF/0/8ff8af940beaf475852560d60046f73f? OpenDocument. (11384)

[180] See: http://domino.un.org/UNISPAL.NSF/0/4080cb55ac61c2658025646c002a89a3? OpenDocument. (11385)

[181] See: http://daccessdds.un.org/doc/UNDOC/GEN/N98/773/11/PDF/N9877311.pdf? OpenElement. (11386)

This document uses extensive links via the Internet. If you experience a broken link, please note the 5 digit number (xxxxx) at the end of the URL and use it as a Keyword in the Search Box at www.MEfacts.com.

It should be noted: The coining of the term "Occupied Palestinian Territory" by the General Assembly, and all the more so its 'adoption' by the International Court of Justice, is contrary to, and *totally incompatible* with, Article 12 of the UN Charter which states:

> "While the Security Council is exercising in respect of any dispute or situation the functions assigned to it in the present Charter, the General Assembly *shall not make any recommendation with regard to that dispute or situation unless the Security Council so requests.*" [italics by author]

International law allows for "just wars" and "lawful occupation."

Resolutions 242 and 338 (discussed in Chapter 9) are the cornerstones for how a "just and lasting peace" should be achieved. The term 'Occupied Palestinian Territory' does not appear in either, not even the term 'occupied territory.' Resolution 242 affirms that:

> "... fulfillment of the Charter principles requires the establishment of a just and lasting peace in the Middle East which should include the application of both the following principles: Withdrawal of Israeli armed forces from territories occupied in the recent conflict; Termination of all claims or states of belligerency and respect for and acknowledgement of the sovereignty, territorial integrity and political independence of every State in the area and their right to live in peace within secure and recognized boundaries free from threats or acts of force."

The ICJ is blissfully unaware that there is such a quality as a "lawful Occupation," discussed elsewhere in this critique. In essence the ICJ seeks to *overturn* Security Council Resolutions 242 and 338, and to de-legitimize Israel's right to claim any territory, over the Green Line, even for self-defence.

In paragraph 74 of the opinion, the ICJ prefers a highly questionable *abridged* rendition of these two core documents in a way that makes it appear as if Israel was an aggressor:

"On 22 November 1967, the Security Council unanimously adopted resolution 242 (1967), which emphasized [E.H. Principle I] the inadmissibility of acquisition of territory by war and [E.H. Principle II] called for the 'Withdrawal of Israel armed forces from territories occupied in the recent conflict,' and [E.H. Principle III] 'Termination of all claims or states of belligerency.'"

ICJ selective writing falsifies historical documents.

The ICJ misleads the readers by simply *removing* from the second principle [Principle II above] the need, as stated in Resolution 242, for "secure and recognized boundaries" that will not invite aggression. In any case, the ICJ cannot override Security Council resolutions nor can it *edit* or *fix* them. Such 'doctored' use of "the inadmissibility of the acquisition of territory by force" is disingenuous, at the very least.

The intention of Resolution 242 is not only reflected in its actual phrasing, which the ICJ crassly distorts. It is anchored in the *type* of Resolution passed by the Security Council.

It is impossible to believe that the ICJ was unfamiliar with the basic rules governing the workings of the UN that are most relevant in understanding the meaning of the Security Council's power and the two types of resolutions it may adopt:

Resolutions adopted under Chapter VI – Recommending "Pacific Resolution of Dispute":

Resolutions the Security Council adopts under Chapter VI are intended to be followed and implemented via negotiated settlements between concerned parties. One of the UN resolutions adopted under Chapter VI of the UN Charter is Resolution 242, adopted in 1967 after the Six-Day War. It calls on Israel and its Arab neighbours to accept the resolution through negotiation, arbitration and conciliation. Under Chapter VI of the UN Charter, the recommendations of UN Resolution 242 cannot *be imposed* on the parties concerned, as Arab leaders often argue. In fact, the title of Chapter VI also offers a clue to its nature, for it deals with "Pacific Resolution of Disputes."

Resolutions adopted under Chapter VII – Dealing with the "Threats to Peace …":

> In contrast, resolutions adopted by the Security Council under Chapter VII invest the Security Council with power to issue stringent resolutions that *require* nations to comply with the terms set forth in the resolution. This leaves no room to negotiate a settlement with the affected parties. Thus, Chapter VII deals with "Threats to Peace, Breaches of the Peace and Acts of Aggression."
>
> When Iraq invaded Kuwait in 1990, the Security Council adopted resolutions under Chapter VII that only required the aggressor, Iraq, to comply.[182]

Had Israel been an aggressor – where the territories were "occupied territories" taken by force in an *unjust* war – Resolution 242 would have been adopted under Chapter VII of the UN Charter, *requiring Israel to comply* … and not under Chapter VI.

In paragraph 26 of its opinion, the ICJ notes that Chapter VII empowers the Security Council to "require enforcement by coercive action," thus *implying* that this Chapter is somehow relevant to this proceedings. Chapter VI isn't even mentioned in the ICJ's opinion – not in general and not with regard to Resolutions 242 or 338, although the Bench cites "242 (1967)" no less than seven times, providing ample opportunity to clarify that 242 adopted under Chapter VI of the UN Charter is intended to be followed and implemented via *negotiated settlements* between the concerned parties and *not by this Court.*

It is important to note here that the ICJ refuses to even acknowledge the existence of scholarly literature that addresses the issue of seizure of territory in *just wars* written by internationally respected, former members of the ICJ. The ICJ simply turns a blind eye to the fact that some wars are *just war* and *not all* occupations are *illegal* – as in the Israeli case, so clearly reflected by the unanimous adoption of UN Security Council Resolution 242 under Chapter VI.

---

[182] UN Security Council Resolution 678, S/RES/0678 (1990), 29 November 1990. See: http://www.mefacts.com/cache/html/icj/11446.htm. (11446)

This document uses extensive links via the Internet. If you experience a broken link, please note the 5 digit number (xxxxx) at the end of the URL and use it as a Keyword in the Search Box at www.MEfacts.com.

As noted earlier, Judge Sir Elihu Lauterpacht, Judge ad hoc of the International Court of Justice, pointed out in a 1968 article (which was also cited by Judge Schwebel in his writings):

> "… territorial change cannot properly take place as a result of the 'unlawful' use of force. But to omit the word 'unlawful' is to change the substantive content of the rule and to turn an important safeguard of legal principle into an aggressor's charter. For if force can never be used to effect lawful territory change, then, if territory has once changed hands as a result of the unlawful use of force, the illegitimacy of the position thus established is sterilized by the prohibition upon the use of force to restore the lawful sovereign. This cannot be regarded as reasonable or correct."[183]

This argument, which is widely recognised, goes unnoticed or is consciously and purposely ignored.

The ICJ's sweeping 'adoption' of General Assembly's resolutions, as if they were legally binding or a source of international law, and the ICJ's unauthorized 'illegal transfer' of unallocated disputed territories to one of the sides in the conflict is all the more ironic in light of the ICJ's main contention: that Israel's actions are primarily political and not security motivated, and that these actions constitute a fait accompli. In paragraph 121 of the opinion the ICJ declares:

> "The Court considers that the construction of the wall and its associated régime create a 'fait accompli' on the ground that could well become permanent, in which case, and notwithstanding the formal characterization of the wall by Israel, it would be tantamount to de facto annexation"

This begs the question: Are the ICJ's own actions in arbitrarily *handing over ownership* and *title* to all territories beyond the Green Line to the Palestinians – including East Jerusalem – not tantamount to unlawful *de facto* annexation?

---

[183] Professor, Judge Sir Elihu Lauterpacht, "Jerusalem and the Holy Places," Pamphlet No. 19 (London, Anglo-Israel Association, 1968).

Professor Stone cites in his writings that in 1975 the ICJ has been:

> "insistent, not least as regards [to] questions of *territorial title,* that the rules and concepts of international law have to be interpreted 'by reference to the law in force' and 'the State practice' at the relevant period. [italics by author]

> "Judge de Castro in his Separate Opinion (ibid., 127, at 168 ff.) declared the principle *tempus regit factum* as a recognized principle of international law. He continued (p. 169): 'Consequently, the creation of ties with or titles to a territory must be determined according to the law in force at the time ... . The rule *tempus regit factum* must also be applied to ascertain the legal force of new facts and their impact on the existing situation.' He went on to illustrate this influence of 'new facts and new law' by reference to the impact on the suppression of the colonial status of Western Sahara by the principles concerning non-self-governing territories emanating from the United-Nations Charter and the later application to them of the principle of Self-determination (pp. 169-71). This limiting rider has reference to the appearance of new principles of international law, overriding the different principles on which earlier titles are based. But, of course, it can have no application to vested titles based, as was the very territorial allocation between the Jewish and Arab peoples, on the principle of self-determination itself."[184]

If the so-called West Bank and Gaza were indeed occupied territory – belonging to someone else and unjustly seized by force – there could be no grounds for negotiating new borders, as UN Security Council Resolution 242 implies.

The ICJ charges that Jewish settlements in the West Bank are populated by settlers 'deported by force.'

Once the ICJ has 'established evidence' that the West Bank and Gaza are unlawfully occupied territories, it then applies this *status* to the Fourth Geneva Conference[185] *de jure*, stating in paragraph 120 of the opinion that:

---

[184] Majority Opinion in the Western Sahara case, I.C.J. Reports, 1975, p. 12, esp. at 38-39) as cited by Professor Julius Stone, "Israel and Palestine, Assault on the Law of Nations." The Johns Hopkins University Press, 1981, p. 127.

[185] Geneva Convention relative to the Protection of Civilian Persons in Time of War. See: http://www.unhchr.ch/html/menu3/b/92.htm. (10356)

This document uses extensive links via the Internet. If you experience a broken link, please note the 5 digit number (xxxxx) at the end of the URL and use it as a Keyword in the Search Box at www.MEfacts.com.

"As regards these settlements, the Court notes that Article 49, paragraph 6, of the Fourth Geneva Convention provides: 'The Occupying Power shall not deport or transfer parts of its own civilian population into the territory it occupies.'

"In this respect, the information *provided to the Court* shows that, since 1977, Israel has conducted a policy and developed practices involving the establishment of settlements in the Occupied Palestinian Territory, contrary to the terms of Article 49, paragraph 6, just cited." [italics by author]

One can hardly believe that the ICJ would come to the baseless conclusion that Israel, the *only* true free democracy in the Middle East, would use "deportation" and "forced transfer" of its own population, actions considered a War Crime by the International Criminal Court.

The Court attempts to 'broaden the definition of Article 49 to possibly 'fit' some wrong doing on the part of the State of Israel, all with no reference to law, adding:

"That provision prohibits not only deportations or forced transfers of population such as those carried out during the Second World War, but also any measures taken by an occupying Power in order to organize or encourage transfers of parts of its own population into the occupied territory."

In the above conclusion, the ICJ fails to disclose the content of the "information provided" (information the Court based its decision-on), and the *anonymous* 'authorities' that provided such. Anyone interested in the subject at hand, is aware of the difficulties the Israeli Government faces in its decision to relocate [disengagement] some Israeli settlements *out* of the "Territories," *a fact* that seems to be contrary to the "information provided" to the ICJ.

Professor Stone touches on the applicability of Article 49 of the Geneva Conventions. Writing on the subject in 1980:

"… that because of the *ex iniuria* principle, Jordan never had nor now has any legal title in the West Bank, nor does any other state even claim such title. Article 49 seems thus simply not applicable. (Even if it were, it may be added that the facts of recent voluntary settlements seem not to be caught by the intent of Article 49 which is rather directed at the forced transfer of the belligerent's inhabitants to the occupied territory, or the displacement of the local inhabitants, for other than security reasons.) The Fourth Geneva Convention applies only, according to Article 2, to occupation of territory belonging to 'another High Contracting Party'; and Jordan cannot show any such title to the West Bank, nor Egypt to Gaza."

Support to Professor Stone's assertion can be found in Judge, Sir Elihu Lauterpacht's writing in 1968:

"Thus Jordan's occupation of the Old City—and indeed of the whole of the area west of the Jordan river—entirely lacked legal justification; and being defective in this way could not form any basis for Jordan validly to fill the sovereignty vacuum in the Old City [and whole of the area west of the Jordan river]."[186]

Professor Eugene V. Rostow, a drafter of UN Security Council Resolution 242 and international law expert, concludes that the Convention is not applicable to Israel's legal position and notes:

"The opposition to Jewish settlements in the West Bank also relied on a legal argument – that such settlements violated the Fourth Geneva Convention forbidding the occupying power from transferring its own citizens into the occupied territories. How that Convention could apply to Jews who already had a legal right, protected by Article 80 of the United Nations Charter, to live in the West Bank, East Jerusalem, and the Gaza Strip, was never explained."[187]

It seems that the International Court of Justice "never explained" it either.

By default, ICJ support of the "Mandate for Palestine" – suggests it is actually supporting Jewish settlement in Palestine. Is the ICJ confused?

The ICJ concluded that under the Fourth Geneva Conference, Jewish settlements in the "Territories" are illegal, which brings up the need to reconcile two of the ICJ's conflicting positions:

---

[186] Professor, Judge Sir Elihu Lauterpacht, "Jerusalem and the Holy Places," Pamphlet No. 19 (London, Anglo-Israel Association, 1968).

[187] Professor Eugene V. Rostow, see: http://www.law.yale.edu/outside/pdf/Public_Affairs/ylr50-2/Rostow.pdf.

The first, as noted above, is the ICJ opinion regarding the *illegal Jewish settlements* in the "Territories."

The second, refers to the ICJ 'adoption' of the "Mandate for Palestine" – a document which under Article 6 testifies to the legality of Jewish settlements in Palestine and does:

> "*encourage,* in co-operation with the Jewish agency referred to in Article 4, [building] *close settlement by Jews* on the land, including State lands and waste lands not required for public purposes."[188] [italics by author]

The ICJ ignores that under international convention[189] and Article 80 of the UN Charter, all of western Palestine is legally open to settlement by Jews and at best the West Bank and Gaza are unallocated territory left over from the British Mandate to which there are two claimants.

Paragraph 88 of the Court's opinion stated that:

> "… the ultimate objective of the sacred trust" referred to in Article 22, paragraph 1, of the Covenant of the League of Nations "was the self-determination … of the peoples concerned"

As we will note both here and later, the ICJ seems confused. It attempts to links the "sacred trust" to the wrong "people concerned"!

UN Charter and Article 80.

International law, the UN Charter, and specifically Article 80 of the UN Charter implicitly recognize the "Mandate for Palestine" of the League of Nations. This Mandate granted Jews the *irrevocable* right to settle in the area of Palestine, anywhere between the Jordan River and the Mediterranean Sea. Professor Eugene V. Rostow, an expert in international law explains:

> "This right is protected by Article 80 of the United Nations Charter. The Mandates of the League of Nations have a special status in international law, considered to be trusts, indeed 'sacred trusts.'

---

[188] See Appendix A "Mandate for Palestine."
[189] Ibid.

"Under international law, neither Jordan nor the Palestinian Arab 'people' of the West Bank and the Gaza Strip have a substantial claim to the sovereign possession of the occupied territories."[190]

It is interesting to learn how Article 80 made its way into the UN Charter. Professor Rostow recalls:

"I am indebted to my learned friend Dr. Paul Riebenfeld, who has for many years been my mentor on the history of Zionism, for reminding me of some of the circumstances which led to the adoption of Article 80 of the Charter. Strong Jewish delegations representing differing political tendencies within Jewry attended the San Francisco Conference in 1945. Rabbi Stephen S. Wise, Peter Bergson, Eliahu Elath, Professors Ben-Zion Netanayu and A. S. Yehuda, and Harry Selden were among the Jewish representatives. Their mission was to protect the Jewish right of settlement in Palestine under the mandate against erosion in a world of ambitious states. Article 80 was the result of their efforts."

The ICJ ignores the history of Jewish life in the area called Palestine.

The ICJ also ignores that Jews who had settled in these areas during almost 30 years of "Mandate" government and, in fact, for thousands of years in some areas such as Hebron and the Old City of Jerusalem (in so-called "East Jerusalem"), in Kfar Darom in Gaza or the Etzion Bloc near Hebron, were either killed or driven out by the Arabs during the 1948 War. All areas of western Palestine that remained under Arab control were rendered racially cleansed of Jews – by Jordanian and Egyptian invaders, an act that in today's parlance would be labeled "ethnic cleansing." Even the 2,000 Jewish inhabitants of the Jewish Quarter of the Old City [of Jerusalem], who lived adjacent to the holiest site to Judaism, the Western Wall in the shadow of the Temple Mount, were an intolerable presence to Arabs.

---

[190] Eugene V. Rostow, "The Future of Palestine" from the paper delivered at the American Leadership Conference on Israel and the Middle East in Arlington, Virginia. October 10 1993. See: http://middleeastfacts.org/content/book/The%20Future%20of%20Palestine.htm. (10509)

While the ICJ opinion mentions Jerusalem 54 times, all references are in relation to Palestinian rights of free access to holy sites, while the ICJ ignores that not one Jew was allowed to reside or even *visit* the West Bank and the Old City of Jerusalem for 19 years of illegal Jordanian rule. Between 1949 and 1967, Jordanian military personnel overran and razed Jewish settlements to the ground, trashed some 58 synagogues, and used headstones from the Mount of Olives cemetery to build roads.[191] After the 1967 Six-Day War, Jews *reestablished* their legal right to settle anywhere in western Palestine – an entitlement unaltered in international law since 1923 and valid to this day.

Invoking the Fourth Geneva Convention to make any Jewish presence in the West Bank, including the Old City of Jerusalem, 'illegal' is hardly applicable – neither from an historical, nor from a legal standpoint.

Where Jews are and are not permitted to settle.

The ICJ chooses to ignore the content of the "Mandate for Palestine" and accompanying legally binding international accords that set the boundaries of the Jewish mandate and delineates where Jews are and are not permitted to settle.

The Court opinion cites in paragraph 70 – almost parenthetically, that

> "The territorial boundaries of the Mandate for Palestine were laid down by various instruments, in particular on the eastern border by a British memorandum of 16 September 1922 and an Anglo-Transjordanian Treaty of 20 February 1928."

The reader is left in the dark as to what these "instruments" say or to what the text refers. No wonder. The ICJ does not quote the content of these two key international treaties and ignores the relevant clauses of the Mandate itself vis-à-vis the status of western Palestine, because citing

---

[191] Jeff Jacoby, "When Jerusalem was divided," see: http://www.mefacts.com/cache/html/territories/11304.htm. (11304)

This document uses extensive links via the Internet. If you experience a broken link, please note the 5 digit number (xxxxx) at the end of the URL and use it as a Keyword in the Search Box at www.MEfacts.com.

these treaties and clauses would collapse the 'foundations' of the commonly-held assumption that Israeli settlements are 'illegal'. It is important to set the record straight. The "eastern border" the ICJ chose not to discuss was the Jordan River.

At first, the six page "Mandate" document did not set the borders – leaving this for the Mandator to stipulate in a binding appendix to the document in the form of a memorandum, but Article 6 of the Mandate says clearly:

> "The Administration of Palestine, while ensuring that the rights and position of other sections of the population are not prejudiced, shall facilitate Jewish immigration under suitable conditions and shall encourage, in co-operation with the Jewish agency referred to in Article 4, *close settlement by Jews on the land, including State lands and waste lands not required for public purposes*". [italics by author]

Article 25 of the "Mandate for Palestine" entitled the Mandatory to change the terms of the Mandate in the part of the Mandate *east* of the Jordan River. That is, it gave the Mandatory an 'escape clause' that was not applicable to western Palestine:

> "In the territories lying between the Jordan and the eastern boundary of Palestine as ultimately determined, the Mandatory shall be entitled, with the consent of the Council of the League of Nations, to postpone or withhold application of such provision of this Mandate as he may consider inapplicable to the existing local conditions ..."[192]

Great Britain activated this option in the above-mentioned memorandum of the 16th of September, 1922 which the Mandatory sent to the League of Nations and which the League subsequently approved – making it a legally binding integral part of the Mandate.

Thus the "Mandate for Palestine" brought to fruition an additional mandate for a fourth Arab state *east* of the Jordan River, realized in 1946 when the Hashemite Kingdom of Transjordan was granted

---

[192] See: Appendix A "Mandate for Palestine."

independence from Great Britain. All the clauses concerning a Jewish homeland would *not* apply to this part (Transjordan) of the original Mandate, stating clearly where this applied:

> "The following provisions of the Mandate for Palestine are not applicable to the territory known as Trans-Jordan, which comprises all territory lying to the east of a line drawn from ... up the centre of the Wady Araba, Dead Sea and River Jordan. ... His Majesty's Government accept[s] full responsibility as Mandatory for Trans-Jordan."

The creation of an Arab state in eastern Palestine (today Jordan), on 76 percent of the land mass of the original Mandate for Jews, in no way changed the status of Jews west of the Jordan River and their right to settle anywhere in western Palestine, between the Jordan River and the Mediterranean Sea.

These documents are the last legally binding documents regarding the status of what is commonly called "the West Bank and Gaza."

The memorandum (regarding Article 25), is also the last modification of the Mandate on record[193] by the League of Nations or by its legal successor – the United Nations – in accordance with Article 27 of the Mandate that states unequivocally:

> "The consent of the Council of the League of Nations is required for any modification of the terms of this mandate."

But to note or to quote these documents would 'spoil' the ICJ's charge that Israeli settlements are "illegal" and that Israel is an unlawful "Occupying Power" of land that 'belongs' to the Arab Palestinians.

The ICJ even uses its own opinions in a selective manner. Under the mistaken assumption that Palestinian self-determination was 'set in stone' by the international community in 1922 by the Mandate for Palestine, the Bench quotes a previous opinion on Namibia that

---

[193] Ibid.

addresses the fate of League of Nations' mandates, stating in paragraph 70 of the opinion:

> "...two principles were considered to be of paramount importance: the principle of non-annexation and the principle that the well-being and development of ... peoples [not yet able to govern themselves] form[ed] 'a sacred trust of civilization'"[194]

The term "sacred trust" quoted by the ICJ is borrowed from the United Nations Charter Article 73[195] which recognizes the UN's commitments of its predecessor – the League of Nations and promises to carry through to fruition the mandate system the League of Nations created, enshrined in Article 22 of the League of Nations Charter. Thus, the Bench quotes from its own 1950 opinion when it believes it supports the Palestinian cause, but the Bench also fails to mention that in the very same decision, it says:

> "... in the case of Namibia, the former South African mandate for the German colony of South West Africa ... *the mandate survived the end of the League of Nations.*" [italics by author]

In other words, since this case (Namibia) is a precedent, neither the ICJ nor the General Assembly can arbitrarily change the status of *Jewish settlement* as set forth in the Mandate for Palestine, an international accord that was never amended.

All of western Palestine, from the Jordan River to the Mediterranean Sea, including the West Bank and Gaza, remains open to Jewish settlement under international law until a legally binding document – in Israel's case, a peace treaty between Arabs and Jews that was called for in Security Resolution 242 and 338, changes this.

---

[194] The latter – a quote from Article 73 of the UN Charter that recognized the League of Nation's mandates as 'non-self-governing territories.'

[195] Charter of the United Nations at: http://middleeastfacts.org/content/UN-Documents/UN_Charter_One_Document.htm. (11032)

This document uses extensive links via the Internet. If you experience a broken link, please note the 5 digit number (xxxxx) at the end of the URL and use it as a Keyword in the Search Box at www.MEfacts.com.

Professor Eugene V. Rostow, position concurred with the ICJ's opinion as to the "sacredness" of such trusts:

> "A trust" – as in Article 80 of the UN Charter (which the Court avoids to mention) – "does not end because the trustee dies" … "the Jewish right of settlement in the whole of western Palestine – the area West of the Jordan – survived the British withdrawal in 1948." … "They are parts of the mandate territory, now legally occupied by Israel with the consent of the Security Council."[196]

The Oslo Accords and the Gaza-Jericho agreements recognizes Israel legal presence in the "Territories" and Israel right to maintain a fence around Gaza.

Even the Oslo Accords recognize the above fact and do not forbid either Israeli (i.e. Jewish) or Arab settlement activity. Likewise, the ICJ does not consider it relevant that the propriety of a *security fence around Gaza* was written into the Gaza-Jericho agreement, between Israel and the PLO, signed in Cairo, May 4, 1994, and that Israel retained the right to provide for security, including the security of Israeli settlers.

> "The Parties agree that, as long as this Agreement is in force, the *security fence erected by Israel around the Gaza Strip* shall remain in place and that the line demarcated by the fence, as shown on attached map No. 1, shall be authoritative only for the purpose of this Agreement."[197] [italics by author]

The ICJ not only rules that Israeli settlements are illegal, based on non-binding General Assembly declarations of *sentiments*; likewise, it views such resolutions as if they were the *Magna Carta* of Palestinian self-determination.

---

[196] Professor Eugene V. Rostow was Sterling Professor of Law and Public Affairs Emeritus at Yale University and served as the Dean of Yale Law School (1955-66); In 1967 as U.S. Under-Secretary of State for Political Affairs he become a key draftee of UN Resolution 242. http://www.mefacts.com/cache/html/bio/10956.htm. (10956)

[197] Gaza-Jericho agreement. See: http://www.mefacts.com/cache/html/arab-peace-agreements/11371.htm (11371)

This document uses extensive links via the Internet. If you experience a broken link, please note the 5 digit number (xxxxx) at the end of the URL and use it as a Keyword in the Search Box at www.MEfacts.com.

The ICJ's narrative of how the Territories came into the possession of Israel is void of any context and sanitized of any trace of past and present Arab aggression.

The backdrop to the 1967 Six-Day War – the expulsion by Egypt of UN peace-keepers from the Sinai Peninsula, Egypt illegal blockade of an international waterway, the massing of Egyptian troops on Israel's borders – mysteriously disappears. The ICJ jumps from the signing of the 1948 armistice agreements that established the Green Line as a temporary border, to the aftermath of the 1967 Six-Day War in *one* step. Paragraph 72 of the opinion recount how:

> "By resolution 62 (1948) of 16 November 1948, the Security Council decided that 'an armistice shall be established in all sectors of Palestine' and called upon the parties directly involved in the conflict to seek agreement to this end. … The Demarcation Line was subject to such rectification as might be agreed upon by the parties."[198]

(It is gratifying that the ICJ notes that the international community never related to the Green Line as a 'sacred' or permanent border, notwithstanding that throughout the opinion, the ICJ certainly seems to view it as such).

Paragraph 73 of the Court's opinion immediately follows, saying:

> "In the 1967 armed conflict, Israeli forces occupied all the territories which had constituted Palestine under British Mandate (including those known as the West Bank, lying to the east of the Green Line)."

Readers might think that Israel just woke up one morning and out of the blue attacked its neighbors and occupied part of their territory without provocation. In fact, both the events and UN resolutions of the period substantiate and recognize that Israel's presence in the West Bank and Gaza is a *legal* occupation.

---

[198] UN Security Council Resolution of 16 November 1948. See: http://domino.un.org/ UNISPAL.NSF/0/1a2b613a2fc85a9d852560c2005d4223?OpenDocument. (11381)

This document uses extensive links via the Internet. If you experience a broken link, please note the 5 digit number (xxxxx) at the end of the URL and use it as a Keyword in the Search Box at www.MEfacts.com.

11 The Supreme Court of the State of Israel

The ICJ's Statute[199] requires it "to decide in accordance with international law." and to apply "... the most highly qualified publicists of the various nations," in this Case, the relevant writings of the Supreme Court of the State of Israel should have been applied "as subsidiary means for the determination of the rules of law."

The ICJ's evaluation of the validity of supporting evidence appears to be carefully tailored to support forgone conclusions. It is the ICJ's own rules that the Bench seems to ignore. Article 38, rule 1(d) of the Court Statute requires that the Court:

> "Shall apply: ... Judicial decisions and the teachings of the most highly qualified publicists of the various *nations* [to] determine rules of law."

The ICJ does not follow the directive in its mandate that requires it to use the most qualified and valued writing of law of other nations – in this case Israel. The Bench not only ignores the rulings of the Supreme Court of the State of Israel that could directly contribute to its own investigation of legality *and* proportionality – discussed below. The

---

[199] Statute of The International Court of Justice at: http://www.icj-cij.org/icjwww/ibasic documents/ibasictext/ibasicstatute.htm. (10485)

This document uses extensive links via the Internet. If you experience a broken link, please note the 5 digit number (xxxxx) at the end of the URL and use it as a Keyword in the Search Box at www.MEfacts.com.

Bench even ignores the writings of former members of its own Bench, including a past president of the Court, as well as a host of other eminent jurists and academic scholars of international law. Nowhere is this more evident than in the way the ICJ addresses findings of the Israeli Supreme Court.

In his writing on *Government Legal Advising in the Field of Foreign Affairs* about what influences and makes international laws, the former president of the International Court of Justice, Judge Schwebel, writes:

> "International law is largely the creation of Governments. In that creative process, those who render legal advice to Governments play a critical part (in present case the Supreme Court of the State of Israel). The forces which shape international law, like the forces which shape international affairs, are many and complex. But what is singular and clear is that those who advise Governments on what international law is and should be exert a particular, perhaps at times a paramount, influence on the formation of international law."[200]

United States Supreme Court Justice Stephen G. Breyer has said that:

> "the United States could learn from compromises Israeli courts have struck to *balance* terrorism and human rights concerns."[201] [italics by author]

At first glance, it would seem that the ICJ recognizes this fact. Closer examination reveals that when convenient, this same Court relies on the Israel Supreme Court to reach a conclusion that *fits* its thinking, but it sees nothing improper in ignoring the most relevant decisions to this case by the Israeli Supreme Court when its findings differ from the ICJ's. Thus, the ICJ supports the applicability of the Hague and Geneva Conventions by citing in paragraph 100 of the ICJ opinion, a May 30, 2004 ruling by the Supreme Court of the State of Israel sitting as a High

---

[200] Professor, Judge Stephen M. Schwebel, *Government Legal Advising in the Field of Foreign Affairs* in "Justice in International Law", Cambridge University Press, 1994. Opinions quoted in this critiques are not derived from his position as a judge of the ICJ.

[201] "Justice: Israeli courts could teach U.S. something about compromise," Associated Press, September 13, 2003. See: http://www.mefacts.com/cache/html/human-rights/10308.htm. (10308)

Court of Justice.[202] The ICJ noted that Israel's highest court of justice ruled that:

> "... the military operations of the [Israeli Defence Forces] in Rafah, to the extent they affect civilians, are governed by Hague Convention IV Respecting the Laws and Customs of War on Land 1907 ... and the Geneva Convention Relative to the Protection of Civilian Persons in Time of War 1949."[203]

Yet when it comes to a far more fundamental question – the purpose of the security fence and whether it is justified in light of the injury it causes Palestinians[204] – the expertise and experience of the Supreme Court of the State of Israel are no longer deemed valid. In paragraph 140 of the ICJ opinion, the Bench declares:

> "... In the light of the material before it, the Court is not convinced that the construction of the wall along the route chosen was the only means to safeguard the interests of Israel against the peril which it has invoked as justification for that construction."

What is 'the highly qualified' material before the ICJ – or to be more precise: Is there highly relevant material that the ICJ arbitrarily judged to be immaterial?

If the Israeli Supreme Court can contribute to the case, why is there no mention whatsoever of a ruling handed down by the Supreme Court of the State of Israel in the case of:

> "Beit Sourik Village Council v. 1. The Government of Israel, (HCJ 2056/04) dated June 30, 2004"[205]

that also recognizes the applicability of the Hague and Geneva Conventions and is also *directly* connected to the security barrier issue?

---

[202] In Hebrew Baggatz.

[203] HCJ 4764/04, May 30, 2004, "Physicians for Human Rights v. Commander of the IDF Forces in the Gaza Strip," at: http://www.mefacts.com/cache/pdf/icj/11387.pdf. (11387)

[204] The wording of the Advisory Opinion does not ask what its ramifications for Israelis are...

[205] HCJ 2056/04, June 30, 2004, "Beit Sourik Village Council v. 1.The Government of Israel," at: http://www.mefacts.com/cache/html/israel/10926.htm. (10926)

This document uses extensive links via the Internet. If you experience a broken link, please note the 5 digit number (xxxxx) at the end of the URL and use it as a Keyword in the Search Box at www.MEfacts.com.

The Case is not hard to find in the online archive of the Israeli Court. In addition, the decision received worldwide exposure, reported internationally in most major media outlets.[206] Moreover, the Israeli Court's Judge Aaron Barak notes in the *opening* paragraph of the second case, the June 30, 2004 ruling:

> "The question before us is whether the orders and the Fence are legal."

Examination of the Israeli Court's ruling reveals why the ICJ *preferred* to quote a ruling that deals with alleged lack of access to medical treatment for civilians in Rafiah in the Gaza Strip in the midst of Israel Defense Forces (IDF) military operations, rather than a ruling that addresses the legality of the *security barrier*, which is on the West Bank, directly relevant to the case.

The Israeli Supreme Court devoted *seven* court sessions to hearing the appeal of *one* Palestinian village that felt it had been wronged by seizure of some of its land to construct the security barrier. The June 30, 2004 judgment is 22,000 words long. The Israeli Court describes at length both the all-pervasive and insidious character of Palestinian terrorism and the injury to Palestinian civilians caused by the security barrier. It concludes in paragraph 28:

> "We examined petitioners' arguments, and have come to the conclusion, based upon the facts before us, that the *Fence is motivated by security concerns.* As we have seen in the government decisions concerning the construction of the Fence, the government has emphasized, numerous times, that '*the Fence, like the additional obstacles, is a security measure.* Its construction does not express a political border, or any other border.' (Decision of June 23, 2002).

> "The obstacle that will be erected pursuant to this decision, like other segments of the obstacle in the Seam Area is a security measure for the prevention of terror attacks and does not mark a national border or any other border." (Government of Israel, decision of October 1, 2003.) [italics by author]

---

[206] See for example *The New York Times*, "Israeli Court Orders Changes to Barrier in West Bank," June 30, 2004, at: http://www.mefacts.com/cache/html/icj/11388.htm. (11388)

This document uses extensive links via the Internet. If you experience a broken link, please note the 5 digit number (xxxxx) at the end of the URL and use it as a Keyword in the Search Box at www.MEfacts.com.

The Israeli high court's ruling doesn't even rate a rebuttal in the ICJ's opinion. It simply does not exist, or it is judged to be immaterial to the case.

It is clear there is *another* reason why the ICJ chose not to highlight this case. On the surface, from the ICJ's point of view, the judgment by the Israeli Court is just as good. It says clearly, in paragraph 23:

> "The authority of the military commander flows from the provisions of public international law regarding belligerent occupation. These rules are established principally in the Regulations Concerning the Laws and Customs of War on Land, The Hague, 18 October 1907 [hereinafter – the Hague Regulations]. These regulations reflect customary international law. The military commander's authority is also anchored in IV Geneva Convention Relative to the Protection of Civilian Persons in Time of War 1949 [hereinafter – the Fourth Geneva Convention]."[207]

But the judgment goes beyond this. The Israeli ruling also *explains* how the Israeli Court views adjudication of appeals for protection under the Hague and Geneva Conventions. In a very lengthy and thoughtful discussion of the challenges facing *any* court, the president of the Israeli Supreme Court says in paragraph 36:

> "The problem of balancing security and liberty is not specific to the discretion of a military commander of an area under belligerent occupation. It is a general problem in the law, both domestic and international. Its solution is universal. It is found deep in the general principles of law, which include reasonableness and good faith. ... One of these foundational principles, which balance the legitimate objective with the means for achieving it, is the principle of proportionality. According to this principle, the liberty of the individual can be limited (in this case, the liberty of the local inhabitants under belligerent occupation), on the condition that the restriction is proportionate. This approach applies to all types of law."

---

[207] Israel Supreme Court, ruling HCJ 2056/04, June 30, 2004, "Beit Sourik Village Council v. 1.The Government of Israel," at: http://www.mefacts.com/cache/html/israel/10926.htm. (10926)

This document uses extensive links via the Internet. If you experience a broken link, please note the 5 digit number (xxxxx) at the end of the URL and use it as a Keyword in the Search Box at www.MEfacts.com.

In paragraph 44, the Israeli Supreme Court adds:

> "The key question regarding the route of the Fence is: Is the route of the Separation Fence proportionate? The proportionality of the Separation Fence must be decided by the three following questions ... First, does the route pass the 'appropriate means' test? ... The question is whether there is a rational connection between the route of the Fence and the goal of the construction of the Separation Fence. Second, does it pass the test of the 'least injurious' means? The question is whether, among the various routes which would achieve the objective of the Separation Fence, is the chosen one the least injurious. Third, does it pass the test of proportionality in the narrow sense? The question is whether the Separation Fence route, as set out by the military commander, injures the local inhabitants to the extent that there is no proper proportion between this injury and the security benefit of the Fence."

For the ICJ to simply quote the Israeli court as 'accepting the applicability of the Hague and Geneva Conventions dealing with behavior towards civilians in wartime' while avoiding explaining what the Israeli court actually means by this, hardly does justice to the Israeli Supreme Court. In fact, such conduct of the ICJ warps the true position of the Israeli court, which demonstrates just how *difficult* it really is to weigh the merits of such a case where the 'right to life' of potential victims of Palestinian terrorism must be balanced against none-lethal injury to Palestinian non-combatants. Such input would be welcome in any fair and judicious Court, but the ICJ, that lacks any military and security experience, and never experienced life under constant terrorism, was not interested in struggling with this issue.

It should be noted in closing that the Supreme Court of the State of Israel and the Government of Israel have as *de facto,* not *de jure,* applied the Hague and Geneva Conferences as a yardstick of humanitarian behavior. The Supreme Court of the State of Israel did not rule that the West Bank and Gaza are occupied territories and certainly has never said they were Occupied Palestinian Territories.

The International Court of Justice distorts the Israeli court's intention.

In paragraph 100 of the ICJ opinion, the Bench mischaracterized the Supreme Court of Israel's limited acceptance of the applicability of Geneva Convention, warping the Israel court's intention and misleading the reader with *selective* use. The Supreme Court of the State of Israel has never suggested that the Geneva Convention applies to the *legal status of Israeli settlers.* Israel signed the Fourth Geneva Convention on August 12, 1949 and ratified it on July 6, 1951. Since then, including after the 1967 war, Israel has not denounced the Convention, as permitted by the convention's Article 158.

As articulated in 1971 by then Attorney General of Israel, Meir Shamgar (who in 1983 became President of the Supreme Court), Israel *voluntarily* abides by the humanitarian provisions of the Geneva Convention in the West Bank and Gaza Strip, despite pointing out that Israel and other world renowned experts of international law believe that the Convention does not apply to these territories *De jure.*

12 Arab Consistent Behavior and Precedent for Fencing

The ICJ ignores the remarkably consistent Arab behavior in Palestine, that is documented in the Mandator's reports to the League of Nations – a role that parallels a UN Special Rapporteur today. Such primary documents contain precedents for security fences and testify to their non-political nature.

The International Court of Justice shows an avid interest in the "Mandate for Palestine" and uses the Mandate document to openly champion a Palestinian state, but the ICJ also chooses to ignore evidence of the 'un-readiness' of Palestinian Arabs for independence – a political maturity that it quotes in the opinion, is a prerequisite for political independence under Article 22 of the League of Nations. Far more crucial to the case: Such documents note the necessity of security barriers in the past and demonstrate that in the context of the Arab-Israeli conflict, indeed, security barriers are temporary in nature. This statement undermines the Bench's opinion that Israel's security fence is political and illegal.

The Bench finds it convenient to ignore that the mandate system speaks of readiness for independence in terms of signs of local responsible governance. As noted at the outset of this critique, Article 22 of the

League of Nation's Charter speaks of reaching "a stage of development" that is provisional "until such time as they are able to stand alone." This yardstick was applied to Lebanon, Iraq, and Syria. By contrast, this ICJ considers Palestinian statehood to be a 'given' – irrespective of Palestinian political behavior.

Ironically, the same political behavior (the use of terrorism as a political instrument) that the ICJ chooses to ignore as irrelevant, is chronicled in official reports to the Council of the League of Nations filed by the British Government during nearly three-decade ruled over Palestine's Arab and Jewish inhabitants.[208] These reports are highly relevant to the case at hand on several counts, but are they admissible? Such reports from the British Government to the Council of the League of Nations were *required* of the Mandator in the terms of the "Mandate for Palestine" in Article 24 it requires that:

> "The Mandatory shall make to the Council of the League of Nations an annual report to the satisfaction of the Council as to the measures taken during the year to carry out the provisions of the mandate. Copies of all laws and regulations promulgated or issued during the year shall be communicated with the report."[209]

Logically, such documents and other special reports to the League by the Mandator should be of equal weight, in terms of standing and credibility, with the reports by the UN special Rapporteur today, such as the one upon which the ICJ opinion says it relies. These reports, as well as the findings of international commissions such as the Anglo-American Committee of Inquiry,[210] could have provided a valuable perspective for the ICJ and placed the current terrorism dilemma in its appropriate historical context.

---

[208] Report by His Majesty's Government in the United Kingdom of Great Britain and Northern Ireland to the Council of the League of Nations on the Administration of Palestine, and by the "Palestine Royal Commission" 1936-1937.

[209] See: Appendix A "Mandate for Palestine."

[210] Report of the Anglo-American Committee of Enquiry Regarding the Problem of European Jewry and Palestine. Lausanne, 20th April, 1946.

Is the Fence a Security measure?

All the more important, the reports are highly relevant in determining whether the fence is a security measure or a political ploy. The ICJ could have learned something about the need for a *security fence* from the Mandate Report of 1930 (p. 169) which noted, after Arabs razed the Jewish farming village of Beer-Tuvia to the ground and attacked ancient Jewish communities in Hebron, Safed and elsewhere in 1929:

> "For the greater security of exposed Jewish *settlements*, the [Jewish] Agency, in co-operation with the [British] Administration, has allotted £P.36,500 to roads, telephones, central buildings and *fencing*." [italics by author]

Seventeen years later, in 1946, the Anglo-American Committee of Enquiry described again, the need for security fences in the face of renewed Arab violence against Jews in 1936-39:

> "The sudden rise of [Jewish] immigration after the Nazi seizure of power had as its direct result the three and a half years of Arab revolt, during which the Jew had to train himself for *self-defence*, and to accustom himself to the life of a pioneer in an armed stockade. ... The high barbed wire and the watchtowers, manned by the settlement police day and night, strike the eye of the visitor as he approaches every collective [Jewish] colony. ... The Jews in Palestine are convinced that Arab violence paid. Throughout the Arab rising, the Jews in the National Home, despite every *provocation, obeyed the orders of their leaders and exercised a remarkable self-discipline*. They shot, *but only in self-defence;* they rarely took reprisals on the Arab population."[211] [italics by author]

Thus, two historical precedents in 1929 and 1936-39 support the Israeli claim that its fencing is not necessarily political or permanent but is a temporary measure prompted by legitimate security needs that ebb and flow like the tide. Indeed, the stockade walls and watchtowers that surrounded isolated civilian Jewish settlements in the later part of the 1930s and protected them from attacks were dismantled when the

---

[211] Report of the Anglo-American Committee of Enquiry regarding the problem of European Jewry and Palestine. Lausanne, 20 April, 1946. Paragraph 7, p. 27.

1936-39 Arab Revolt subsided. This challenges the Court's conclusion that the fence is "political", "de facto annexation" and unilaterally changes the status of parts of the West Bank, all without any reference to law.

The Report by His Majesty's Government in the United Kingdom of Great Britain and Northern Ireland to the Council of the League of Nations on the Administration of Palestine and the Palestine Royal Commission 1936-1937 – testifies to the fact that there is no linkage between terrorism and "occupation" and the use of violence that required building security fences is not new. Unfortunately, these are salient features on the landscape that repeat themselves due to the violence deeply embedded in Palestinian political culture. The only difference is that the 'shoe is on the other foot' in terms of 'who is fenced in,' the potential victims or the perpetrators.

The above Mandator's report definitively cites its corroborative evidence:

> "There were similar assaults [by the Arabs] on the persons and property of the Jews, conducted with the same reckless ferocity. Women and children were not spared. ... In 1936 this was still clearer. Jewish lives were taken and Jewish property destroyed. ... The word 'disturbances' gives a misleading impression of what happened. It was an open rebellion of the Palestinian Arabs, assisted by fellow Arabs from other countries, against British Mandatory rule. Throughout the strike the Arab press indulged in unrestrained invective against the [British] Government. The [British] Government imprisons and demolishes [houses] and imposes extortionate fines in the interests of imperialism."[212]

The British report to the League of Nations had no problem using the 'T' word or acknowledging the sustaining character of political violence in Palestinian Arab culture – internal and external, noting:

> "The ugliest element in the picture remains to be noted. Arab nationalism in Palestine has not escaped infection with the foul disease which has so often

---

[212] British National Archive, Palestine Royal Commission report, July 1937, Chapter IV, p. 104.

defiled the cause of nationalism in other lands. Acts of 'terrorism' in various parts of the country have long been only too familiar reading in the newspapers. As in Ireland in the worst days after the War or in Bengal, intimidation at the point of a revolver has become a not infrequent feature of Arab politics. Attacks by Arabs on Jews, unhappily, are no new thing. The novelty in the present situation is attacks by Arabs on Arabs. For an Arab to be suspected of a lukewarm adherence to the nationalist cause is to invite a visit from a body of 'gunmen.'"[213]

The British report to the League of Nations noted Palestinian Arabs "refusal to negotiate"

"The Arab leaders had refused to co-operate with us [E.H. British] in our search for a means of settling the [E.H. Arab-Jewish] dispute."[214]

The British report to the League of Nations noted the hate that fueled Palestinian Arab political culture:

"…in Palestine Arab nationalism is inextricably interwoven with antagonism to the Jews. … That is why *it is difficult to be an Arab patriot and not to hate the Jews.*" [italics by author]

"…we [E.H. The British] find ourselves reluctantly convinced that no prospect of a lasting settlement can be founded on moderate Arab nationalism. At every successive crisis in the past that hope has been entertained. In each case it has proved illusory."[215] [italics by author]

The British report to the League of Nations noted the destructive role of Palestinian Arab leadership:

"If anything is said in public or done in daylight against the known desires of the Arab Higher Committee, it is the work not of a more moderate, but a *more full-blooded nationalism* than theirs [AHC]."[216] [italics by author]

---

[213] Ibid. Chapter V, Paragraph 45, p. 135.

[214] Ibid. Chapter V, "The Present Situation", Paragraph 1, p. 113.

[215] Ibid. Chapter V, "3. Arab Nationalism", Paragraph 37, p. 131.

[216] Ibid. Chapter V, Paragraph 39, p. 132.

13 Self-Determination

A rogue state "… puts a high priority on subverting other states and sponsoring non-conventional types of violence against them. It does not react predictably to deterrence or other tools of diplomacy and statecraft."[217]

The ICJ opinion cites the right to self-determination as a fundamental right almost two dozen times, always in the Palestinian context, never in the Jewish framework.

The Bench even takes the liberty to *interpret* what Israel's recognition of "Palestinian rights" in a legally-binding accord (Camp David) meant, basing its own interpretation on a declarative statement of *sentiment* by the United Nation's General Assembly. With no reliance on legal standing, the ICJ is saying in paragraph 118:

> "The Israeli-Palestinian Interim Agreement on the West Bank and the Gaza Strip of 28 September 1995 also refers a number of times to the Palestinian people and its 'legitimate rights.' … The Court considers that those rights include the right to self-determination, as the General Assembly has moreover recognized on a number of occasions (see, for example, resolution 58/163 of 22 December 2003)."

---

[217] Barry Rubin, "US Foreign Policy and Rogue States," MERIA, September 1999, at: http://www.biu.ac.il/SOC/besa/meria/journal/1999/issue3/jv3n3a7.html.(11389)

This document uses extensive links via the Internet. If you experience a broken link, please note the 5 digit number (xxxxx) at the end of the URL and use it as a Keyword in the Search Box at www.MEfacts.com.

Again, the ICJ turns General Assembly *recognition* - this time a December 2003 Resolution recognizing "The right of Palestinian people to self-determination"[218] – into the basis for a legal opinion, ignoring the powers vested (or not vested, as the case may be) in the General Assembly under the UN Charter.

It is instructive to compare such 'instant recognition' to the way the Jewish people's right to self-determination, totally ignored by the ICJ, was anchored in a series of *genuine* international accords.

The British objectives in 'mentoring' a national home for the Jewish people' under the Mandate for Palestine were not based solely on the 1917 Balfour Declaration. While international support for the establishment of a Jewish homeland in Palestine was set in motion by this landmark British policy statement, international intent rested on a solid consensus, expressed in a series of accords and declarations that reflected the 'will' of the international community, hardly the product or whim of a colonial empire with its own agenda.

The Mandate itself notes this intent when it cites that the Mandate is based on the agreement of "*the Principal Allied Powers*" and declares:

> "*Whereas recognition has therefore been given* to the historical connection of the Jewish people with Palestine and *to the grounds for* reconstructing their national home in that country" [italics by author].

A June 1922 letter from the British Secretary of State for the Colonies, Winston Churchill, reiterated that

> "...the [Balfour] Declaration of 1917 [was] re-affirmed by the Conference of the Principle Allied Powers at San Remo and again in the Treaty of Sevres" ... "the Jewish people ... is in Palestine as a right and not on sufferance. That is the reason why it necessary that the existence of a Jewish National Home in Palestine should be internationally guaranteed, and that it should be formally recognized to rest upon ancient historical connection."

---

[218] UN General Assembly - 58/163. A/RES/58/163. 77th plenary meeting. 22 December 2003. The right of the Palestinian people to self-determination. See: http://www.mefacts. com/cache/html/un-resolutions/11319.htm. (11319)

This document uses extensive links via the Internet. If you experience a broken link, please note the 5 digit number (xxxxx) at the end of the URL and use it as a Keyword in the Search Box at www.MEfacts.com.

In his first Report of The High Commissioner on the Administration of Palestine 1920-1925 To the Secretary of State for the Colonies, published in April 1925, the most senior official of the Mandate for Palestine, the High Commissioner for Palestine, underscored how "international guarantee[s]" for the existence of a Jewish National Home in Palestine were achieved:

> "The Declaration was endorsed at the time by several of the Allied Governments; it was reaffirmed by the Conference of the Principal Allied Powers at San Remo in 1920; it was subsequently endorsed by unanimous resolutions of both Houses of the Congress of the United States; it was embodied in the Mandate for Palestine approved by the League of Nations in 1922; it was declared, in a formal statement of policy issued by the Colonial Secretary in the same year, 'not to be susceptible of change;' and it has been the guiding principle in their direction of the affairs of Palestine of four successive British Governments. The policy was fixed and internationally guaranteed."

It is remarkable to note the Report of The High Commissioner on the Administration of Palestine to the Right Honourable L. S. Amery, M.P., Secretary of State for the Colonies' Government Offices in 22nd April, 1925, describing Jewish peoplehood:

> "During the last two or three generations the Jews have recreated in Palestine a community, now numbering 80,000, of whom about one-fourth are farmers or workers upon the land. This community has its own political organs, an elected assembly for the direction of its domestic concerns, elected councils in the towns, and an organisation for the control of its schools. It has its elected Chief Rabbinate and Rabbinical Council for the direction of its religious affairs. Its business is conducted in Hebrew as a vernacular language, and a Hebrew press serves its needs. It has its distinctive intellectual life and displays considerable economic activity. This community, then, with its town and country population, its political, religious and social organisations, its own language, its own customs, its own life, has in fact 'national' characteristics.

> "When it is asked what is meant by the development of the Jewish National Home in Palestine, it may be answered that it is not the imposition of a Jewish nationality upon the inhabitants of Palestine as a whole, but the further development of the existing Jewish community, with the assistance of Jews in other parts of the world, in order that it may become a centre in which the Jewish people as a whole may take, on grounds of religion and

race, an interest and a pride. But in order that this community should have the best prospect of free development and provide a full opportunity for the Jewish people to display its capacities, it is essential that it should know that it is in Palestine as of right and not on sufferance. That is the reason why it is necessary that the existence of a Jewish National Home in Palestine should be internationally guaranteed, and that it should be formally recognised to rest upon ancient historic connection."

Eleven successive British governments, Labor and Conservative, from David Lloyd George (1916-1922) through Clement Attlee (1945-1952) viewed themselves as duty-bound to fulfill the "Mandate for Palestine" placed in the hands of Great Britain by the League of Nations.[219]

This is a far cry from the *instant approval* noted in the UN's General Assembly upon which the ICJ bases its findings, totally ignoring that at no point in the "Mandate for Palestine" is there any granting of *political* rights to non-Jewish entities (i.e. Arabs), only *civil* rights (discussed in Chapter 2), because political rights to self-determination as a polity for Arabs were guaranteed in four other parallel mandates for Arab peoples, initially – in Lebanon, Syria, Iraq – and later, Transjordan.

There is one more point that should be mentioned at this juncture: the ICJ's highly irregular perception of peoplehood, eligibility and readiness for self-determination. In paragraph 118 the ICJ says:

"As regards the principle of the right of peoples to self-determination, the Court observes that the existence of a 'Palestinian people' is no longer in issue. ... The Israeli-Palestinian Interim Agreement on the West Bank and the Gaza Strip of 28 September 1995 (Oslo II Accords) also refers a number of times to the Palestinian people and its 'legitimate rights.'"

Making its judgment, the ICJ concludes:

"The Court considers that those rights include the right to self-determination, as the General Assembly has moreover recognized on a number of occasions."

---

[219] See http://www.direct.gov.uk/Homepage/fs/en.

Professor Rostow, examining the claim for Palestinian's self-determination on the bases of law, concludes:

> "… the mandate implicitly denies Arab claims to national political rights in the area in favor of the Jews; the mandated territory was in effect reserved to the Jewish people for their self-determination and political development, in acknowledgment of the historic connection of the Jewish people to the land. Lord Curzon, who was then the British Foreign Minister, made this reading of the mandate explicit. There remains simply the theory that the Arab inhabitants of the West Bank and the Gaza Strip have an inherent 'natural law' claim to the area.
>
> Neither customary international law nor the United Nations Charter acknowledges that every group of people claiming to be a nation has the right to a state of its own." [220]

---

[220] Eugene V. Rostow, "The Future of Palestine," Institute for National Strategic Studies, November 1993. See also his writing: "Are Israel's Settlements Legal?" *The New Republic*, October 21, 1991.

14 The International Court of Justice's 'Mandate'

At all too many junctures it appears that the ICJ's conclusions are based solely on 'gut feelings' and unsubstantiated assumptions – almost taking a leap of faith based on a mixture of personal and collective prejudice and popular opinion.

Article 38 of the ICJ's own Statute instructs the Bench what input is to be applied in adjudicating cases in its Docket.[221] Article 38 clarifies:

> "1. The Court, whose function is to decide in accordance with international law such disputes as are submitted to it, shall apply:
>
> "a. international conventions, whether general or particular, establishing rules expressly recognized by the contesting states;
>
> "b. international custom, as evidence of a general practice accepted as law;
>
> "c. the general principles of law recognized by civilized nations;

---

[221] Statute of the International Court of Justice. See http://www.icj-cij.org/icjwww/ibasic documents/ibasictext/ibasicstatute.htm. (10485)

This document uses extensive links via the Internet. If you experience a broken link, please note the 5 digit number (xxxxx) at the end of the URL and use it as a Keyword in the Search Box at www.MEfacts.com.

"d. subject to the provisions of Article 59, judicial decisions and the teachings of the most highly qualified publicists of the various nations, as subsidiary means for the determination of rules of law."

Throughout this critique of the ICJ's performance of its duties, the Bench has been found time after time to be biased in application of the above-mentioned foundations of international law.

1(a) *International Conventions:* The Bench applies international conventions that are applicable and inapplicable, while ignoring others that are highly relevant, demonstrating a total disregard or lack of understanding of the UN's own legal machinery by treating General Assembly resolutions as if they were legally valid and/or legally binding documents.

It is not even clear whether international conventions are admissible as evidence in an Advisory Opinion: The wording of Article 38 views as admissible only "international conventions, whether general or particular, … expressly recognized by the contesting states." This seems to indicate that in terms of *fair use,* the ICJ is mandated only to use general conventions such as the Hague and Geneva Conventions and the human rights conventions cited by the ICJ (as well as equally relevant ones the ICJ chose not to cite) *only* in cases where the ICJ *is sitting in the capacity of an arbitrator between two sides where both sides* have accepted its jurisdiction. Therefore, use of general conventions might *not apply* when the ICJ has been asked for an advisory opinion – all the more so because Israel, the only "state" in the case, clarified in its brief to the ICJ that it did not accept the court's jurisdiction.

1(b) *International Custom:* The Bench often perverts the general principles of law – the core elements which include reasonableness, good faith and the principle of proportionality, components that are highly relevant to the case at hand, which pits Palestinian rights against Israeli rights.

Furthermore, the rules of war enshrined in the Hague (1907) and Geneva Conventions (1949) did not envision terrorism as a major form of warfare.[222] Until a comprehensive use of convention or protocol on terrorism is established and takes force, countries like America that respect the rule of law have taken the lead to fill the void by defining a new category for such terrorists – 'illegal combatants'. This category, the United States argues, recognizes that one cannot abridge all the rules of warfare by targeting civilians and then expect to enjoy the privileges of POWs under the same conventions. The ICJ prefers to rigidly stick to outdated definitions that hardly reflect current realities about terrorism.

Security barriers in other disputed territories.

Moreover, Israel is not the only country in the world with a security barrier in disputed territory. If the ICJ has been requested to examine the legality and the ramifications of the Israeli barrier and if realities in South West Africa (Namibia) are considered by the ICJ to be relevant to the case at hand, then logically the legality and ramifications of a barrier just up the coast in Western Sahara and also built inside disputed territory would be relevant to the case. Israel is not only *singled out* in the General Assembly request, but also by the ICJ, which exhibits no interest in even noting the existence of precedents or using them as a yardstick of proportionality. The two most outstanding cases are Morocco in the disputed territory of the Western Sahara and India in the disputed territory of Kashmir.

Even without going into the intricacies of the conflicts, a few facts are enlightening: In 1982, Morocco began building a 1,500 kilometer-long defensive wall to protect its settlers and military personnel against Polisario guerrillas – members of the Saharawi tribes who claimed title to the Western Sahara and demanded self-determination. Morocco claims the Western Sahara is an integral part of pre-colonial Morocco.

---

[222] Amnon Straschnov, "Israel's Commitment to Domestic and International Law in Times of War," JCPA, October 10, 2004, at: http://www.jcpa.org/brief/brief4-5.htm. (11390)

This document uses extensive links via the Internet. If you experience a broken link, please note the 5 digit number (xxxxx) at the end of the URL and use it as a Keyword in the Search Box at www.MEfacts.com.

The barrier consists of a series of berms (3 meter high sand walls) deep inside the disputed territory – each between 300 – 670 kilometers in length, seeded with an estimated 200,000 to one million[223] anti-personal and anti-vehicle mines planted in a 100 meter-wide strip on the 'enemy' side of Morocco's security barrier.[224]

In the late 1980s, India began building a security fence to protect itself from Sikh separatists supported by Pakistan; the barrier runs the full length of India's Rajasthan and Punjab states. In 2003, in the wake of cross-border attacks into the Indian sector of the disputed territory of Kashmir by Islamic terrorists, India begun extending the existing 8-foot high mud wall with a 3-tier maze of barbed-wire[225] into the disputed territory, along a route that runs deep inside Kashmir. The planned 1,800 mile security fence, like Israel's, is non-lethal – comprised of steel posts set into concrete blocks and strung up with concertina wire.

1(c) *General Principles of Law of Civilized Nations:* It is hard to justify the ICJ's failing to even discuss crimes against humanity such as systematic targeting of civilians by suicide bombers or the Court's failure to consider the human rights conventions it quotes as being equally applicable to Jews and Arabs.

The instructions to the ICJ that it apply the "general principles of law of civilized nations" raises a far more fundamental question, a matter of propriety. Common decency should have led this ICJ Bench to at least bar those with blood on their hands from participating in such a procedure.

---

[223] Estimates vary between 200,000 and one million mines. See "Landmines – A Threat Still Lingering," at: http://wsahara.net/landmines.html. (11391)

[224] "Desert Dreams, Saharan Nightmares: Morocco, Polisario and the Struggle for Western Sahara" at: http://www.wibemedia.com/sahara.html (11392) for general information and use of mining as a part of the barrier see: http://www.icbl.org (11393) and http://www.icbl.org/lm/2002/western_sahara/. (11394)

[225] Rama Lakshmi, "India's Border Fence Extended to Kashmir," Washington Post, July 30, 2003 at: http://www.washingtonpost.com/ac2/wp-dyn?pagename=article&node=&contentId=A64700-2003Jul29&notFound=true. (11464)

Legal scholar Professor Stone, writing about Palestinian attempts to *resurrect* the 'Partition Plan' (discussed in Chapter 4), wrote:

> "... there are also certain other legal grounds, rooted in basic notions of justice and equity, on which the Arab states (and the Palestinians whom they represented in these matters) should not, in any case, be permitted, after so lawless a resort to violence against the plan, to turn around decades later, and claim legal entitlements under it. More than one of 'the general principles of law' acknowledged in Article 38(1)(c) of the Statute of the International Court of Justice seem to forbid it. Such claimants do not come with 'clean hands' to seek equity; their hands indeed are mired by their lawlessly violent bid to destroy the very resolution and plan from which they now seek equity ..."[226]

If this is so, it is hard to ignore the relevance of "clean hands" in the eligibility of Palestine to seek redress from the ICJ, or at least for bodies such as the PLO, Fatah, the Arab League and the Conference of Islamic States who champion and sanction violence, to aid the ICJ by "furnishing it with information." If this doesn't violate "basic notions of justice and equity," than barring Israeli victims from testifying surely does.

The ICJ did not consider it fitting and proper to invite the Organization of Casualties of Terror Acts in Israel (Almagor) to present evidence under the 'catch-all' Article 66 Clause 2 of its Charter invoked to listen to the Arab League. A request on the part of Israeli terror victims' families to participate in oral hearings was rejected by the ICJ on the grounds that the families do not represent a country and therefore should not take part in the hearings.[227]

1(d) *Judicial decisions:* "Judicial decisions and the teachings of the most highly qualified publicists of the various nations," ... [to] determine rules of law.

---

[226] Professor Julius Stone, "Israel and Palestine, Assault on the Law of Nations" The Johns Hopkins University Press, 1981, p. 127.

[227] "ICJ rejects terror victim's families participation," *Jerusalem Post*, February 21, 2004 at: http://www.jpost.com/servlet/Satellite?pagename=JPost/JPArticle/Printer&cid=10773514 68319. (11486)

The Bench not only ignores the relevant rulings of the Supreme Court of the State of Israel that truly could contribute to its own investigation of legality *and* proportionality – discussed above – but even ignores the writings of former members of its own Bench, Judge Schwebel, who wrote specifically to this omission as noted before in this critique:

> "International law is largely the creation of Governments. In that creative process, those who render legal advice to Governments play a critical part (in present case the Supreme Court of the State of Israel). The forces which shape international law, like the forces which shape international affairs, are many and complex. But what is singular and clear is that those who advise Governments on what international law is and should be exert a particular, perhaps at times a paramount, influence on the formation of international law."[228]

The International Court of Justice is prohibited from considering declarations and resolutions of the General Assembly in its opinions.

To understand what the ICJ cannot do, it is instructive to review the language used during the debate of the defeated draft resolution that attempted to allow the ICJ to consider *declarations* and *resolutions* of the UN General Assembly as if they were customary international law:

> "… complete imbalance" is what Professor Stone describes the "arising from the entry of scores of new states into the United Nations promotes resolutions in the General Assembly reflecting political, economic, or sociological aspirations rather than a responsible assessment of the relevant legal issues and considerations. It would greatly enhance the dangers inherent in this imbalance in the United Nations, if the above illusion were thoughtlessly indulged."

---

[228] Professor, Judge Stephen M. Schwebel, *Government Legal Advising in the Field of Foreign Affairs* in "Justice in International Law", Cambridge University Press, 1994. Opinions quoted in this critiques are not derived from his position as a judge of the ICJ.

Professor Stone continue to describe the 1974 rejected attempt to *over empower* the ICJ:

> "... at the 1492d meeting of the General Assembly's Sixth Committee, on November 5, 1974. ... The Committee had before it a draft resolution on the role of the International Court of Justice, the preamble of which referred vaguely in its eighth paragraph to the possibility that the court might take into consideration declarations and resolutions of the General Assembly. A wide spectrum of states, including Third World, Soviet bloc, and Western states, rejected even this indecisive reference. It was, some said, an attempt at 'indirect amendment' of Article 38 of the Statute of the International Court - a 'subversion of the international structure of the United Nations'"[229]

An ICJ that welcomed the arguments of a master terrorist such as Yasser Arafat, but gives no weight to the words and opinions of former members of the Court, and turns a deaf ear to Israeli victims of terror, and cites declarations and resolutions of the General Assembly as a source of customary international law, can only be held in contempt of its own mandate.

---

[229] (Mr. Sette Camara [Brazil] United Nations General Assembly [U.N.G.A.] A/C6/SR1492, p. 166, with whom U.S. representative Rosenstock agreed on this point). It contradicted the U.N. Charter and the court Statute, so that on a separate vote the Soviet Union would not have supported it (Mr. Fedarov, Union of Soviet Socialist Republics, ibid., p. 167). It was capable of meaning that "General Assembly resolutions could themselves develop international law" (Mr. Steel, for United Kingdom, ibid., p. 167). It was "inappropriate in the light of Article 38" of the Court's Statute (Mr. Guney, Turkey, ibid., p. 168). It was subject to "serious doubts" (Mrs. Ulyanova, Ukraine, ibid., p. 168). It was an attempt to "issue directives regarding the sources of law," departing from his delegation's view that resolutions and declarations of the General Assembly are "essentially recommendations and not legally binding" (Mr. Yokota, Japan, ibid., p. 168). Mr. Rasoloko, Byelorussia, declared roundly (ibid., p. 169) that "declarations and resolutions of the General Assembly could not be sources of international law"; and Mr. Prieto, Chile (ibid., p. 169) added that they could not be so considered "particularly in view of their increasing political content which was often at variance with international law." The eighth paragraph, it was also objected, attributed to the General Assembly "powers which were not within its competence" (Mr. Foldeak, Hungary, ibid., p. 169). Also, the preambular paragraph in question had already been amended at the instance of Mexico in a sense explained as in no way altering or introducing any new source of international law to those enumerated in Article 38 of the Statute of the International Court of Justice (A/C6/L 989).

When rendering an Advisory Opinion, the International Court of Justice has no authority to issue a directive to Member States, a function reserved only to the Security Council.

In paragraph 163 (3)D the Opinion states:

> "All States are under an obligation not to recognize the illegal situation resulting from the construction of the wall and not to render aid or assistance in maintaining the situation created by such construction; all States parties to the Fourth Geneva Convention relative to the Protection of Civilian Persons in Time of War of 12 August 1949 have in addition the obligation, while respecting the United Nations Charter and international law, to ensure compliance by Israel with international humanitarian law as embodied in that Convention;"

Such a directive goes beyond the authority of the Court on three counts. First, no directive was requested of the Court by the UN General Assembly. Just as the Court decided on its own to 'rule' on the legality of Jewish settlements in Section 120 (see Chapter 10), an issue not requested by the General Assembly. Secondly, the Court's powers under its own mandate do not include the right to issue directives to enforce its Advisory Opinion. Just as General Assembly's resolutions are only recommendations, the Court's Advisory Opinion – is also void of any legislative or coercive power, and are no more than counsel or advice. Thirdly, adoption and enforcement of the ICJ's advice is solely the prerogative of the Security Council, the only UN organ with the power under the UN Charter to 'direct' or 'obligate' Member States how to act.

Here again, the Court's behaviour seems either to be propelled by over-eagerness to do its Master's bidding in using the UN judicial system to divest Israel of its rights, or is a sheer 'power grab' reflecting the Bench's own aspirations to assume prerogatives reserved solely for the Security Council, in order to bring the ICJ's own powers into parity with those of the Security Council.

15 Epilogue

In December 2003, Israel-bashing at the United Nations took a new and dangerous turn, including for the first time, the UN's *judicial* machinery. A coalition dominated by oppressive regimes at the General Assembly requested an advisory opinion from the International Court of Justice (ICJ) regarding the "legality" of the security barrier Israel built to impede the movements of suicide bombers from the West Bank into Israel and the "ramifications" of the barrier (on Palestinians only).

For many reasons, the International Court of Justice's Advisory Opinion on Israel's security barrier does not deserve to be dignified by a learned rebuttal. It merits the same treatment as another shameful United Nations document – the 1975 General Assembly Resolution 3379 that equated Zionism with racism.[230] Israel's ambassador to the UN, the late Haim Herzog, tore up the insidious document from the General Assembly's podium. Almost 30 years later, in July 2004, the ICJ 'joined forces' with the UN Secretary-General and the UN General Assembly, to hand down an 'Opinion' that is:

---

[230] The resolution was repealed in 1991, but the terminology continues to reverberate throughout the UN halls and other UN resolutions. See Resolution A/RES/46/86. (11487)

This document uses extensive links via the Internet. If you experience a broken link, please note the 5 digit number (xxxxx) at the end of the URL and use it as a Keyword in the Search Box at www.MEfacts.com.

So *biased* that it found terrorist activities to be irrelevant to its judicial investigation.

So *sloppy* that it leads the reader to assume that the 1922 "Mandate for Palestine" was the founding document for Arab Palestinian self-determination rather than an instrument which detailed the legal system for an internationally-mandated Jewish homeland in Palestine.

So *incompetent* that it demonstrates a total disregard or lack of understanding of the UN's own legal machinery by treating General Assembly Resolutions and Declarations as legally valid and/or legally binding documents.[231]

So *manipulative* that it 'found' in this case a "failure of the Security Council to discharge its responsibilities,"[232] then in defiance of the limited powers delegated to it by the UN Charter, by-passed the Security Council's powers and responsibilities.

This last issue should *alarm* all members of the Security Council, and the United States in particular. It is part of a broader campaign. Nabil Elaraby, the Egyptian member of the ICJ Bench, openly advocates two main vehicles for institutionalizing such prerogatives:

> "The United Nations membership should, in my view, address ways and means to render the Security Council (a) accountable to the General Assembly, and (b) subject to the possibility, however remote, of a judicial review process."[233]

---

[231] "… at the 1492d meeting of the General Assembly's Sixth Committee, on November 5, 1974." See footnote 229 on page 143.

[232] The Court cites UN GA Resolution 377 of 3 November 1950 as its license to assume the Security Council Power. [E.H. The UN Charter vests no such power in GA Resolutions.] (11399)

[233] Nabil Elaraby, "Some Reflections on The Role of the Security Council and the Prohibition of the Use of Force in International Relations: Article 2(4) Revisited in Light of Recent Developments," 2003, at http://edoc.mpil.de/fs/2003/eitel/41_elaraby.pdf. (11449) Not a lone voice, the same sentiments are echoed in Ahmad Faiz bin Abdul Rahman, "The ICJ on Trial" at: http://www.iol.ie/~afifi/BICNews/Afaiz/afaiz21.htm, (11448) who in 1998 took the ICJ to task for not "practice[ing] its powers of judicial review to the fullest extent" in the case brought by Libya against the UK and the United States regarding jurisdiction in the Lockerbie case.

This document uses extensive links via the Internet. If you experience a broken link, please note the 5 digit number (xxxxx) at the end of the URL and use it as a Keyword in the Search Box at www.MEfacts.com.

According to the legal advisor to the PLO Gregory Khalil, in the security barrier case, the ICJ consciously sought to engage:

> "… the United States in a tango of mutual deterrence" and "chart a path for the international community to counter the United States' veto power." The significance of the ruling cannot be overstated, he underscores: It challenges the power of the veto and the Security Council's management of "threats to world peace," using the International Court of Justice's interpretations of the rule of international law in matters of 'threats to world peace" coupled with claims that the international community is *obliged* to support its rulings and calling for sanctions – decisions that under Chapter VII of the UN Charter is the sole prerogative of the Security Council. Khalil calls this strategy "vetoing the veto."[234]

The ICJ ignores not only its own Statute, but also the writings of eminent jurists and academic scholars of international law, members of its *own* Bench, including a past president of the ICJ, all of whom are uniquely qualified and experienced on the subject at hand. Among them: Professor and Judge Stephen M. Schwebel, past president of the ICJ; Sir Gerald Fitzmaurice, former ICJ judge; Judge Sir Hersch Lauterpacht, a former member judge of the International Court; Judge Sir Elihu Lauterpacht, judge ad hoc of the International Court of Justice; former British Ambassador to the UN, Lord Caradon, principal author of draft Resolution 242; Professor Julius Stone, one of the 20th century's leading authorities on the Law of Nations; Professor Eugene V. Rostow, dean of the Yale Law School, U.S. Under-Secretary of State for Political Affairs, and a key draftee of UN Resolution 242; Professor and Jurist Arthur J. Goldberg, member of the U.S. Supreme Court, and U.S. Ambassador to the UN in 1967 and a key draftee of Resolution 242; and Professor George P. Fletcher, faculty member of the Columbia

---

[234]   See Gregory Khalil, "Just Say No to Vetoes," New York Times, July 19, 2004, at http://www.pngo. net/publications/articles/gregory_khalil190704en.htm. (11450)

This document uses extensive links via the Internet. If you experience a broken link, please note the 5 digit number (xxxxx) at the end of the URL and use it as a Keyword in the Search Box at www.MEfacts.com.

University School of Law, who recently wrote: "Kofi Annan's use of the phrase 'illegal occupation' is a "perilous threat to the diplomatic search for peace."[235]

The ICJ's opinion requires attention because of its potential *use and abuse* by Israel's and America's adversaries, now and in the future, who enjoy an automatic majority vote in the General Assembly, and who seek to undermine "World Order" as we know it.

The ruling is a breakthrough event in interpretation of international law, threatening the security of the United States and the war on terrorism. American legislators and policymakers need to take note and appropriate action.

The Opinion on Israel's security barrier is part of a larger effort to alter the power matrix inside the UN and in the world community, including challenges to the balance between politics and law.[236] It is not merely a problem for Israel, nor is it a passing episode.

The Opinion written by the Court's president Shi Jiuyong[237] constitutes "a profound corruption of its mission and one with seismic implications

---

[235] "Kofi Annan's use of the phrase 'illegal occupation' is a 'perilous threat to the diplomatic search for peace,'" Professor George Fletcher, an expert in international law at Columbia University School of Law and author of "Romantics at War: Glory and Guilt in the Age of Terrorism." See "Annan's Careless Language," *The New York Times*, March 21, 2002. (10327)

[236] This includes attempts to expand 'universal jurisdiction,' make all aspects of politics subject to international adjudication and generally 'put law above politics.' It 'wishes' to reform the UN in a manner that would strip the Security Council of its 'undemocratic' powers.

[237] "The court president, Shi Jiuyong, hails from China, one of the more dictatorial regimes in the world ... continues to deny basic political and religious rights, with large numbers of dissidents held in prisons and labor camps for 'crimes' such as advocating free elections or practicing the Falun Gong religion. Israel, needless to say, has complete freedom of speech and religion. And, while Israel wants to annex only a small sliver of the West Bank, China has grabbed all of Tibet. But, with its veto power at the U.N. Security Council, Beijing is able to shield itself from well-deserved international obloquy." See: Andrew McCarthy, "The End of the Right of Self-Defense: Israel, the World Court, and the War on Terror," Commentary, November 1, 2004 at: http://www.defenddemocracy.org/in_the_media/in_the_media_show.htm?doc_id=245738. (10447)

This document uses extensive links via the Internet. If you experience a broken link, please note the 5 digit number (xxxxx) at the end of the URL and use it as a Keyword in the Search Box at www.MEfacts.com.

for the future of international law."[238] It threatens American security on two levels: *first*, in its groundbreaking attack on the 'right to self-defense' proscribing an *almost blanket prohibition of use of lawful force*, and *second*, in the willingness of the Bench to allow its chambers to become a *political instrument* and to abandon all semblance of fairness or professionalism, for political gain.

This critique focused on the Court's *competence* as reflected in the contents of the Opinion – the quality and relevance of the documentation it chose to quote (or ignore), and the misuse (or no use) of 'law.' Examination of the ICJ's 62-page Opinion reveals just how far the Bench was willing to go to serve political ends. The opinion was not only rife with bias, but also *consciously engaged in gross misuse of historical facts, documentation and the rule of law.*

Consequently, the issues and the threats demand a far more serious, systematic and frank response – including *a willingness to challenge the competence of the ICJ, and this Bench in particular.*

This critique's findings should be read by all concerned with the competence of the Court, and should be shared with the widest possible audience. Attempts to 'shield' the Court from this disgrace, out of concern for its perceived reputation and effectiveness are short-sighted, to say the least.

Only exposure can help undo some of the damage, and to help ensure that there will be no 'repeat performance' … next time with the United States in the Docket perhaps. Other steps need to be taken to engage the 'universal jurisdiction' and the 'law above politics' camps in a serious debate of the issues. Until then we need the General Assembly and the International Court of Justice to step beyond their respective mandates, and to respect and obey international laws as set forth in the United Nations Charter.

---

[238] Ibid.

No distinction rest between Genocide and the undoing of the State of Israel by the International Court of Justice at the Hague. To suggest denying Israel's right for self-defense in favor of Palestinian's incommode and Palestinian's terrorism, is a crime against humanity.

LEAGUE OF NATIONS

MANDATE FOR PALESTINE,

TOGETHER WITH A

NOTE BY THE SECRETARY - GENERAL
RELATING TO ITS APPLICATION

TO THE

TERRITORY KNOWN AS TRANS-JORDAN,

under the provisions of Article 25.

================================

Presented to Parliament by Command of His Majesty,
December, 1922.

================================

LONDON:
PUBLISHED BY HIS MAJESTY'S STATIONARY OFFICE.

MANDATE FOR PALESTINE,

together with a Note by the Secretary-General relating to its application to the Territory known as Trans-Jordan, under the provisions of Article 25.

MANDATE FOR PALESTINE.

The Council of the League of Nations :

Whereas the Principal Allied Powers have agreed, for the purpose of giving effect to the provisions of Article 22 of the Covenant of the League of Nations, to entrust to a Mandatory selected by the said Powers the administration of the territory of Palestine, which formerly belonged to the Turkish Empire, within such boundaries as may be fixed by them; and

Whereas the Principal Allied Powers have also agreed that the Mandatory should be responsible for putting into effect the declaration originally made on November 2nd, 1917, by the Government of His Britannic Majesty, and adopted by the said Powers, in favor of the establishment in Palestine of a national home for the Jewish people, it being clearly understood that nothing should be done which might prejudice the civil and religious rights of existing non-Jewish communities in Palestine, or the rights and political status enjoyed by Jews in any other country; and

Whereas recognition has thereby been given to the historical connection of the Jewish people with Palestine and to the grounds for reconstituting their national home in that country; and

Whereas the Principal Allied Powers have selected His Britannic Majesty as the Mandatory for Palestine; and

Whereas the mandate in respect of Palestine has been formulated in the following terms and submitted to the Council of the League for approval; and

Whereas His Britannic Majesty has accepted the mandate in respect of Palestine and undertaken to exercise it on behalf of the League of Nations in conformity with the following provisions; and

Whereas by the afore-mentioned Article 22 (paragraph 8), it is provided that the degree of authority, control or administration to be exercised by the Mandatory, not having been previously agreed upon by the Members of the League, shall be explicitly defined by the Council of the League of Nations;

confirming the said Mandate, defines its terms as follows:

Article 1.

The Mandatory shall have full powers of legislation and of administration, save as they may be limited by the terms of this mandate.

Article 2.

The Mandatory shall be responsible for placing the country under such political, administrative and economic conditions as will secure the establishment of the Jewish national home, as laid down in the preamble, and the development of self-governing institutions, and also for safeguarding the civil and religious rights of all the inhabitants of Palestine, irrespective of race and religion.

Article 3.

The Mandatory shall, so far as circumstances permit, encourage local autonomy.

Article 4.

An appropriate Jewish agency shall be recognised as a public body for the purpose of advising and co-operating with the Administration of Palestine in such economic, social and other matters as may affect the establishment of the Jewish national home and the interests of the Jewish population in Palestine, and, subject always to the control of the Administration to assist and take part in the development of the country.

The Zionist organization, so long as its organization and constitution are in the opinion of the Mandatory appropriate, shall be recognised as such agency. It shall take steps in consultation with His Britannic Majesty's Government to secure the co-operation of all Jews who are willing to assist in the establishment of the Jewish national home.

Article 5.

The Mandatory shall be responsible for seeing that no Palestine territory shall be ceded or leased to, or in any way placed under the control of the Government of any foreign Power.

Article 6.

The Administration of Palestine, while ensuring that the rights and position of other sections of the population are not prejudiced, shall facilitate Jewish immigration under suitable conditions and shall encourage, in co-operation with the Jewish agency referred to in Article 4, close settlement by Jews on the land, including State lands and waste lands not required for public purposes.

Article 7.

The Administration of Palestine shall be responsible for enacting a nationality law. There shall be included in this law provisions framed so as to facilitate the acquisition of Palestinian citizenship by Jews who take up their permanent residence in Palestine.

Article 8.

The privileges and immunities of foreigners, including the benefits of consular jurisdiction and protection as formerly enjoyed by Capitulation or usage in the Ottoman Empire, shall not be applicable in Palestine.

Unless the Powers whose nationals enjoyed the afore-mentioned privileges and immunities on August 1st, 1914, shall have previously renounced the right to their re-establishment, or shall have agreed to their non-application for a specified period, these privileges and immunities shall, at the expiration of the mandate, be immediately re-established in their entirety or with such modifications as may have been agreed upon between the Powers concerned.

Article 9.

The Mandatory shall be responsible for seeing that the judicial system established in Palestine shall assure to foreigners, as well as to natives, a complete guarantee of their rights.

Respect for the personal status of the various peoples and communities and for their religious interests shall be fully guaranteed. In particular, the control and administration of Wakfs shall be exercised in accordance with religious law and the dispositions of the founders.

Article 10.

Pending the making of special extradition agreements relating to Palestine, the extradition treaties in force between the Mandatory and other foreign Powers shall apply to Palestine.

Article 11.

The Administration of Palestine shall take all necessary measures to safeguard the interests of the community in connection with the development of the country, and, subject to any international obligations accepted by the Mandatory, shall have full power to provide for public ownership or control of any of the natural resources of the country or of the public works, services and utilities established or to be established therein. It shall introduce a land system appropriate to the needs of the country, having regard, among other things, to the desirability of promoting the close settlement and intensive cultivation of the land.

The Administration may arrange with the Jewish agency mentioned in Article 4 to construct or operate, upon fair and equitable terms, any public works, services and utilities, and to develop any of the natural resources of the country, in so far as these matters are not directly undertaken by the Administration. Any such arrangements shall provide that no profits distributed by such agency, directly or indirectly, shall exceed a reasonable rate of interest on the capital, and any further profits shall be utilised by it for the benefit of the country in a manner approved by the Administration.

Article 12.

The Mandatory shall be entrusted with the control of the foreign relations of Palestine and the right to issue exequaturs to consuls appointed by foreign Powers. He shall also be entitled to afford diplomatic and consular protection to citizens of Palestine when outside its territorial limits.

Article 13.

All responsibility in connection with the Holy Places and religious buildings or sites in Palestine, including that of preserving existing rights and of securing free access to the Holy Places, religious buildings and sites and the free exercise of worship, while ensuring the requirements of public order and decorum, is assumed by the Mandatory, who shall be responsible solely to the League of Nations in all matters connected herewith, provided that nothing in this article shall prevent the Mandatory from entering into such arrangements as he may deem reasonable with the Administration for the purpose of carrying the provisions of this article into effect; and provided also that nothing in this mandate shall be construed as conferring upon the Mandatory authority to interfere with the fabric or the management of purely Moslem sacred shrines, the immunities of which are guaranteed.

Article 14.

A special commission shall be appointed by the Mandatory to study, define and determine the rights and claims in connection with the Holy Places and the rights and claims relating to the different religious communities in Palestine. The method of nomination, the composition and the functions of this Commission shall be submitted to